The Kali Linux Handbook

A Practical Guide to Advanced Cybersecurity Techniques

Oliver O'Neill

Welcome to "**The Kali Linux Handbook: A Practical Guide to Advanced Cybersecurity Techniques**." In this comprehensive book, we embark on a thrilling journey through the world of Kali Linux, an essential and powerful tool for modern cybersecurity professionals and enthusiasts alike. Whether you are a seasoned penetration tester, a curious student, or an IT professional seeking to fortify your organization's security defenses, this handbook is designed to equip you with the knowledge and skills needed to master the art of cybersecurity using Kali Linux.

Chapter by chapter, we will dive into the depths of Kali Linux, exploring its vast array of tools, methodologies, and real-world applications. From the fundamental principles of ethical hacking to the intricacies of advanced network exploitation, each chapter is thoughtfully crafted to provide you with hands-on experience and expert guidance. Our goal is to empower you to safeguard critical assets, identify vulnerabilities, and counteract potential cyber threats effectively.

Unleashing the Power of Kali Linux

Why Kali Linux?

As the de facto standard for penetration testing and ethical hacking, Kali Linux stands tall as a versatile, open-source platform designed to cater to the ever-evolving challenges of cybersecurity. With its rich repository of specialized tools and a robust community backing, Kali Linux allows you to wield the same powerful techniques utilized by professional cybersecurity experts worldwide.

Who is this Book For?

This handbook is intended for anyone with a passion for cybersecurity, regardless of their level of expertise. Whether you are just starting on your cybersecurity journey or you have years of experience under your belt, you will find valuable insights and practical knowledge within these pages. For beginners, we offer a gentle introduction to the essential concepts, while more seasoned professionals can delve into advanced methodologies and real-world case studies.

How to Use This Handbook

Each chapter is carefully structured to build upon the knowledge gained from the previous one, allowing for a seamless learning experience. However, feel free to jump to specific topics of interest, as every chapter is designed to stand on its own. Each section is enriched with examples, step-by-step instructions, and hands-on exercises, enabling you to reinforce your understanding of the concepts presented.

A Note on Ethics

As you embark on your journey through the world of cybersecurity, it is crucial to remember the ethical implications of your actions. The tools and techniques discussed in this book are potent and can be misused for nefarious purposes. We emphasize the importance of using this knowledge responsibly and legally. Ethical hacking aims to improve security, protect valuable assets, and safeguard privacy, rather than causing harm or disruption.

Get Ready to Dive In!

As we set forth on this expedition, be prepared to unlock the full potential of Kali Linux and discover the excitement of mastering advanced cybersecurity techniques. Together, we will explore the ever-changing landscape of cybersecurity, arm ourselves with cutting-edge tools, and develop the skills to protect, defend, and outmaneuver potential adversaries.

Let us embark on this adventure, embracing the challenges and opportunities that lie ahead. Welcome to "The Kali Linux Handbook: A Practical Guide to Advanced Cybersecurity Techniques." Let's begin this transformative journey together.

Chapter 1: Introduction to Kali Linux

Welcome to the first chapter of "The Kali Linux Handbook: A Practical Guide to Advanced Cybersecurity Techniques." In this chapter, we embark on an exciting journey into the world of Kali Linux, a versatile and powerful operating system specifically designed for cybersecurity professionals and enthusiasts.

The Evolution of Kali Linux

As we delve into the depths of Kali Linux, we begin by tracing its evolution and understanding the driving forces behind its creation. Originally born from the BackTrack Linux project, Kali Linux has grown into a leading platform for ethical hacking, penetration testing, and vulnerability assessment. We'll explore how the passionate cybersecurity community contributed to its development, shaping it into the indispensable tool it is today.

Understanding Cybersecurity Landscape

In an increasingly interconnected world, the need for robust cybersecurity has never been more critical. In this section, we shed light on the ever-evolving cybersecurity landscape, exploring the prevalent threats and challenges faced by organizations and individuals alike. Understanding the adversaries and potential vulnerabilities lays the groundwork for why Kali Linux and ethical hacking are essential components of modern cybersecurity defenses.

Setting Up a Virtual Environment

Before we begin our hands-on exploration of Kali Linux, we need to set up a safe and controlled environment to practice our cybersecurity techniques. In this part, we guide you through the process of creating a virtual environment using popular virtualization platforms. By doing so, you can experiment and experiment without the fear of impacting real-world systems.

Installing Kali Linux

In this section, we provide a detailed walkthrough of the Kali Linux installation process. Whether you choose to install it on a physical machine or a virtual environment, we will cover the essential steps to get your Kali Linux instance up and running smoothly. Additionally, we discuss various installation options and considerations to tailor Kali Linux to your specific needs.

As we begin our journey with Kali Linux, let us embrace the spirit of ethical hacking and responsible exploration. Understanding the history, significance, and installation of Kali Linux sets the stage for the exciting chapters ahead. So, fasten your seatbelt and get ready to embark on an adventure into the world of advanced cybersecurity techniques, empowered by the remarkable capabilities of Kali Linux.

Happy hacking and learning!

1.1 The Evolution of Kali Linux

Kali Linux, a powerful and versatile operating system built for cybersecurity professionals and enthusiasts, has a rich and fascinating evolution that traces its roots back to the early days of the information security community. In this essay, we will explore the journey of Kali Linux, from its humble beginnings to becoming the go-to platform for ethical hacking and penetration testing.

1.1.1 The Origins of Kali Linux

To understand the origins of Kali Linux, we must first delve into the history of its predecessor, BackTrack Linux. BackTrack Linux was a Linux distribution created by Mati Aharoni and Max Moser, released in 2006. It gained rapid popularity due to its exceptional collection of security tools and ease of use. The security community embraced BackTrack for its ability to perform various cybersecurity tasks, such as penetration testing, vulnerability assessment, and digital forensics.

1.1.2 The Birth of Kali Linux

As BackTrack Linux evolved, it faced challenges in terms of maintaining a stable and reliable codebase. Recognizing these limitations, the creators decided to rebuild the entire distribution from scratch, which led to the birth of Kali Linux. In 2013, Offensive Security, a cybersecurity training and penetration testing company, took over the development and management of Kali Linux, with Mati Aharoni and Devon Kearns playing key roles.

The goal of creating Kali Linux was to address the shortcomings of BackTrack and provide a more robust and efficient platform for cybersecurity professionals. By rebuilding the distribution with a solid Debian base and incorporating improved infrastructure, Kali Linux aimed to become the most comprehensive and cutting-edge toolset for ethical hackers and security researchers.

1.1.3 The Kali Linux Philosophy

Kali Linux was built upon a foundation of principles and philosophy that distinguished it from other Linux distributions. Its primary focus was on providing a single, unified platform that encompassed all the necessary tools for cybersecurity professionals. Rather than creating separate tools, Kali Linux aimed to integrate a vast collection of powerful applications, simplifying the setup and maintenance for security practitioners.

Open-source collaboration was at the heart of Kali Linux's development. The community's contribution was highly encouraged, and various ethical hacking and cybersecurity experts participated in improving and expanding the distribution's capabilities. This spirit of collaboration ensured that Kali Linux stayed at the forefront of cybersecurity tools, continuously evolving to meet the demands of the ever-changing landscape.

1.1.4 The Rise to Prominence

Kali Linux's feature-rich toolset, combined with its user-friendly interface and extensive documentation, quickly gained popularity within the cybersecurity community. Its capabilities extended beyond penetration testing to include areas such as digital forensics, reverse engineering, and wireless security assessment. As a result, Kali Linux became a go-to platform for security professionals, students, and enthusiasts alike.

Additionally, Kali Linux's adaptability and portability contributed to its widespread adoption. It was designed to run on various hardware architectures and could be installed on physical machines, virtual environments, and even mobile devices. This flexibility made Kali Linux accessible to a wide range of users, ensuring its position as a leading cybersecurity toolset.

1.1.5 Kali Linux Releases and Updates

One of the key factors in Kali Linux's success is its dedication to continuous improvement. Offensive Security maintained a regular release schedule, ensuring that the distribution remained up-to-date with the latest security tools and software updates. Frequent updates and patches allowed users to stay ahead of emerging threats and vulnerabilities.

Moreover, Kali Linux's vast repository of pre-configured tools was organized into various categories, simplifying navigation and allowing users to quickly find the specific tools they needed for their tasks. This well-structured approach enhanced productivity and efficiency for cybersecurity practitioners.

1.1.6 The Impact on Cybersecurity Education

As Kali Linux gained popularity, it also made a significant impact on cybersecurity education. Educational institutions and training programs integrated Kali Linux into their curriculums to provide hands-on experience with real-world cybersecurity scenarios. By using Kali Linux in a controlled and ethical environment, students could develop practical skills and become adept at addressing cybersecurity challenges.

Furthermore, Kali Linux's extensive documentation and online resources, along with a thriving community of users and developers, provided invaluable support to those learning about ethical hacking and penetration testing. The availability of free and accessible educational resources played a crucial role in nurturing the next generation of cybersecurity professionals.

1.1.7 Kali Linux Today

In the present day, Kali Linux stands as a testament to the collaborative efforts of the cybersecurity community. Its reputation as a comprehensive and powerful cybersecurity toolset remains unparalleled. Offensive Security's commitment to constant improvement and maintaining the distribution's high standards has solidified Kali Linux's position as the premier platform for ethical hacking and cybersecurity assessments.

The future of Kali Linux continues to be bright, as the cybersecurity landscape continues to evolve, and new threats and challenges emerge. As technology advances, Kali Linux will undoubtedly adapt and innovate to meet the needs of cybersecurity professionals and remain at the forefront of ethical hacking and penetration testing.

In conclusion, the evolution of Kali Linux from its origins as BackTrack Linux to its current status as a leading cybersecurity platform showcases the power of open-source collaboration and the dedication of the cybersecurity community. Its impact on cybersecurity education and the broader cybersecurity industry is undeniable, making Kali Linux an indispensable tool for those seeking to secure digital landscapes and defend against emerging cyber threats.

1.2 Understanding Cybersecurity Landscape

The cybersecurity landscape is a dynamic and ever-evolving domain that encompasses the protection of digital assets, data, and systems from malicious attacks, unauthorized access, and potential threats. In this section, we will explore the key components and challenges that shape the cybersecurity landscape, as well as the critical role of cybersecurity in today's interconnected world.

1.2.1 The Digital Transformation

The rapid advancement of technology has led to a digital transformation, where almost every aspect of modern life is connected to the digital realm. From personal devices like smartphones and smartwatches to critical infrastructures such as power grids and financial systems, digital technologies have become an integral part of our daily lives.

While this digital revolution has brought numerous benefits and conveniences, it has also exposed us to new and complex cybersecurity challenges. The interconnectedness of devices and systems creates a vast attack surface for cybercriminals, making it essential to secure every entry point effectively.

1.2.2 The Proliferation of Cyber Threats

The cybersecurity landscape is plagued by an ever-increasing number of cyber threats. Cybercriminals continuously develop sophisticated techniques to exploit vulnerabilities and gain unauthorized access to sensitive information. These threats range from traditional malware, such as viruses and worms, to more advanced and targeted attacks, including ransomware, advanced persistent threats (APTs), and zero-day exploits.

Moreover, the rise of nation-state cyber-espionage and cyberwarfare has added a new dimension to the cybersecurity landscape. State-sponsored actors engage in sophisticated cyber operations to steal sensitive information, disrupt critical infrastructures, and conduct acts of sabotage against rival nations.

1.2.3 The Importance of Data Protection

In the digital age, data has become one of the most valuable assets for individuals and organizations alike. Protecting sensitive data from unauthorized access and breaches is a top priority for cybersecurity professionals. Data breaches can result in severe consequences, such as financial losses, reputational damage, and legal liabilities.

Cybersecurity efforts often focus on implementing robust data encryption, access controls, and secure data storage practices. Additionally, the emerging field of data privacy and compliance requires organizations to adhere to strict regulations and guidelines for handling personal and sensitive data.

1.2.4 The Role of Human Factors

While technological advancements are crucial for cybersecurity, human factors also play a significant role in the cybersecurity landscape. Human errors, such as weak passwords, falling victim to social engineering attacks, or failing to keep software up to date, can open doors for cyber attackers.

To address this challenge, cybersecurity professionals must emphasize cybersecurity awareness and training for individuals at all levels of an organization. Educating users about common cybersecurity risks and best practices can significantly reduce the likelihood of successful cyberattacks.

1.2.5 The Evolving Regulatory Environment

The ever-changing regulatory environment adds complexity to the cybersecurity landscape. Governments and regulatory bodies worldwide are enacting new laws and regulations to address the growing cybersecurity threats and protect consumer data privacy.

For instance, the European Union's General Data Protection Regulation (GDPR) has established strict rules for data protection and privacy, with severe penalties for non-compliance. Similarly, other countries have implemented their own cybersecurity laws, creating a global patchwork of regulations that organizations must navigate to remain compliant.

1.2.6 The Role of Cybersecurity Professionals

In the face of these challenges, the role of cybersecurity professionals has become increasingly critical. Ethical hackers, cybersecurity analysts, incident responders, and other specialists are on the front lines of defending against cyber threats.

Cybersecurity professionals continuously monitor networks for suspicious activities, perform penetration testing and vulnerability assessments, and respond to security incidents promptly. Their expertise is invaluable in identifying and mitigating security risks, protecting digital assets, and ensuring the resilience of systems and infrastructures.

1.2.7 The Need for Collaboration

The cybersecurity landscape requires a collaborative effort from all stakeholders, including governments, businesses, educational institutions, and individuals. Cybersecurity threats know no borders, and effective defense requires cooperation on a global scale.

Information sharing and collaboration among organizations, cybersecurity vendors, and government agencies are essential for developing threat intelligence and understanding emerging cyber threats. Additionally, public-private partnerships can foster innovation and the development of new cybersecurity technologies and practices.

In conclusion, the cybersecurity landscape is a complex and ever-changing domain shaped by technological advancements, cyber threats, data protection concerns, human factors, regulatory developments, and the role of cybersecurity professionals. As technology continues to evolve, so will the cybersecurity landscape, requiring constant adaptation and collaboration to stay ahead of emerging threats and protect digital assets effectively.

1.3 Setting Up a Virtual Environment

A virtual environment is a crucial tool for cybersecurity professionals and enthusiasts, providing a safe and isolated space to conduct various cybersecurity tasks, including penetration testing, vulnerability assessment, and malware analysis. In this section, we will explore the process of setting up a virtual environment using virtualization software, allowing users to run multiple operating systems simultaneously on a single physical machine.

1.3.1 Virtualization Software

Virtualization software enables the creation and management of virtual machines (VMs) on a host system. There are several popular virtualization software options, including:

Oracle VirtualBox: A free and open-source virtualization software suitable for individual users and small-scale deployments.

VMware Workstation and VMware Player: Commercial virtualization solutions that offer advanced features and scalability.

Microsoft Hyper-V: A built-in virtualization feature for Windows operating systems, available on specific editions of Windows.

For the purpose of this guide, we will use Oracle VirtualBox as it is widely used, user-friendly, and available on multiple platforms.

1.3.2 Installing VirtualBox

To set up a virtual environment using VirtualBox, follow these steps:

Download VirtualBox: Visit the official VirtualBox website (https://www.virtualbox.org) and download the appropriate version of VirtualBox for your operating system.

Install VirtualBox: Run the installer and follow the on-screen instructions to install VirtualBox on your system.

Download Operating System ISOs: Obtain the ISO images of the operating systems you wish to use in your virtual environment. For example, you may want to use Kali Linux, Windows, Ubuntu, or other Linux distributions.

1.3.3 Creating a Virtual Machine

After installing VirtualBox, follow these steps to create a virtual machine:

Open VirtualBox: Launch the VirtualBox application.

Click "New": Click on the "New" button to start creating a new virtual machine.

Name and Operating System: Enter a name for your virtual machine and select the type of operating system you will be installing (e.g., Linux, Windows, etc.). VirtualBox will automatically adjust some settings based on your selection.

Memory Allocation: Choose the amount of RAM (memory) to allocate to the virtual machine. Ensure that you have enough RAM available on your host system to accommodate the virtual machine's needs without impacting its performance.

Virtual Hard Disk: Create a virtual hard disk for the virtual machine. You can choose to create a new virtual hard disk or use an existing one. It is recommended to select the dynamically allocated option, as it allows the virtual hard disk to grow as needed.

File Location and Size: Specify the location on your host system where the virtual hard disk file will be stored and set its size. The size can be adjusted later if needed.

Finish: Review the virtual machine settings and click "Create" to create the virtual machine.

1.3.4 Installing the Operating System

With the virtual machine created, it's time to install the operating system:

Select the Virtual Machine: In VirtualBox, select the virtual machine you just created from the list of available VMs.

Start the Virtual Machine: Click the "Start" button to launch the virtual machine. VirtualBox will prompt you to select an installation medium. Choose the ISO image of the operating system you wish to install.

Follow the OS Installation Wizard: The virtual machine will boot from the selected ISO image, and the operating system's installation process will begin. Follow the on-screen instructions to install the OS just as you would on a physical machine.

Install Guest Additions (Optional): After installing the OS, you may want to install VirtualBox Guest Additions, which provide additional features and better integration between the host and virtual machine. Instructions for installing Guest Additions are available in the VirtualBox documentation.

1.3.5 Running Multiple Virtual Machines

Once you have set up one virtual machine, you can create additional virtual machines to run different operating systems or to simulate network configurations. To do so, follow the steps outlined in the "Creating a Virtual Machine" section for each new VM you wish to create.

1.3.6 Networking in Virtual Machines

By default, VirtualBox creates a NAT network interface for virtual machines, allowing them to access the internet through the host system's network connection. However, you may want to set up custom network configurations, such as bridged networking or internal networking, to simulate specific network scenarios.

To configure networking in VirtualBox, go to the "Settings" of a virtual machine and navigate to the "Network" tab. From there, you can choose the desired network mode and configure additional network adapters or port forwarding if needed.

1.3.7 Snapshot and Cloning (Optional)

VirtualBox offers powerful features like snapshots and cloning. Snapshots allow you to capture the current state of a virtual machine, enabling you to revert to that state if needed. Cloning allows you to create exact duplicates of virtual machines, making it easy to set up multiple identical test environments.

These optional features can be valuable when experimenting with various configurations or when you need to preserve specific states for future use.

In conclusion, setting up a virtual environment using VirtualBox provides cybersecurity professionals with a safe and flexible space to conduct various cybersecurity tasks. By creating virtual machines for different operating systems and network configurations, users can simulate real-world scenarios, perform ethical hacking and penetration testing, and experiment with cybersecurity tools without impacting their host systems.

1.4 Installing Kali Linux

Kali Linux is a specialized Linux distribution designed for penetration testing and ethical hacking. In this section, we will guide you through the process of installing Kali Linux on a virtual machine using Oracle VirtualBox. This method allows you to run Kali Linux alongside your existing operating system, providing a safe and isolated environment for cybersecurity activities.

1.4.1 Downloading Kali Linux ISO

Before starting the installation process, you need to obtain the Kali Linux ISO image:

Visit the Kali Linux website: Go to the official Kali Linux website at https://www.kali.org and navigate to the "Downloads" section.

Choose the appropriate version: Select the version of Kali Linux that matches your system's architecture (e.g., 64-bit or 32-bit).

Download the ISO: Click on the download link to save the Kali Linux ISO image to your computer.

1.4.2 Creating a New Virtual Machine

Now that you have the Kali Linux ISO, follow these steps to create a new virtual machine for Kali Linux:

Open VirtualBox: Launch the VirtualBox application on your computer.

Click "New": Click on the "New" button to create a new virtual machine.

Name and Operating System: Enter a name for your virtual machine (e.g., "Kali Linux") and select "Linux" as the type. Choose "Debian (64-bit)" as the version since Kali Linux is based on Debian.

Memory Allocation: Allocate an appropriate amount of RAM to your virtual machine. For Kali Linux, a minimum of 2 GB is recommended, but more RAM will improve performance.

Virtual Hard Disk: Choose the option to "Create a virtual hard disk now" and click "Create."

Hard Disk File Type: Select "VDI (VirtualBox Disk Image)" as the file type and click "Next."

Storage on Physical Hard Disk: Choose the "Dynamically allocated" option, which allows the virtual hard disk to grow in size as needed.

File Location and Size: Specify the location on your computer where the virtual hard disk file will be stored and set its size. A size of at least 20 GB is recommended for a basic Kali Linux installation.

Finish: Review the settings and click "Create" to create the virtual machine.

1.4.3 Configuring the Virtual Machine

With the virtual machine created, it's time to configure it for Kali Linux:

Select the Virtual Machine: In VirtualBox, select the virtual machine you just created from the list of available VMs.

Click "Settings": Click on the "Settings" button to access the virtual machine's configuration.

Storage Settings: In the settings window, navigate to the "Storage" tab. Click on the "Empty" optical drive and then click the small disk icon on the right to choose a disk file. Select the Kali Linux ISO image you downloaded earlier.

Network Settings: In the settings window, navigate to the "Network" tab. Ensure that the "Adapter 1" is set to "NAT," which allows the virtual machine to access the internet through the host system's network connection.

Start the Virtual Machine: Click "OK" to save the settings and return to the main VirtualBox window. Select the Kali Linux virtual machine and click "Start" to launch the virtual machine.

1.4.4 Installing Kali Linux

Now that the virtual machine is booted from the Kali Linux ISO, follow these steps to install Kali Linux:

Boot from ISO: The Kali Linux installer will load, and you will be presented with a boot menu. Choose the "Graphical Install" option to begin the installation process.

Language Selection: Select your preferred language for the installation process.

Location and Keyboard: Choose your location and keyboard layout.

Network Configuration: Enter a hostname for your Kali Linux system and configure the domain name if applicable.

Set Root Password: Set a password for the root (administrator) account. Ensure that it is strong and secure.

User Account: Create a regular user account with a strong password.

Time Zone Configuration: Select your time zone.

Disk Partitioning: Choose the disk partitioning method that suits your needs. For beginners, the guided option is recommended.

Write Changes to Disk: Review the partitioning changes and confirm to write them to the disk.

Install GRUB Boot Loader: Choose "Yes" to install the GRUB boot loader.

Installation Complete: Once the installation is complete, the system will prompt you to remove the installation media (ISO). Follow the instructions to remove the ISO image.

Boot into Kali Linux: Restart the virtual machine. After the reboot, you will be prompted to log in with the user account you created during the installation.

1.4.5 Updating Kali Linux

After installing Kali Linux, it is essential to update the system to ensure that you have the latest security patches and software updates. Open a terminal and run the following commands:

sudo apt update
sudo apt upgrade

1.4.6 Optional: Installing VirtualBox Guest Additions

To improve the integration between the host and the virtual machine, you may want to install VirtualBox Guest Additions. Guest Additions provide additional features, such as better display resolution and shared folders.

To install VirtualBox Guest Additions, click on "Devices" in the VirtualBox menu while the Kali Linux virtual machine is running and choose "Insert Guest Additions CD image." Then, follow the on-screen instructions to install the Guest Additions.

In conclusion, setting up Kali Linux in a virtual environment provides a safe and isolated platform for cybersecurity activities. By installing Kali Linux on a virtual machine, you can experiment with various security tools, perform penetration testing, and learn ethical hacking techniques without impacting your primary operating system.

Chapter 2: Basic Kali Linux Commands

Welcome to Chapter 2 of "The Kali Linux Handbook: A Practical Guide to Advanced Cybersecurity Techniques." In this chapter, we dive into the fundamental building blocks of Kali Linux—the command-line interface (CLI) and the essential commands that empower you to interact with this powerful operating system.

Navigating the Terminal

The command-line interface is the heart of Kali Linux, providing direct access to its vast capabilities. In this section, we familiarize ourselves with the terminal and learn how to navigate the file system efficiently. You'll gain confidence in using commands to list directories, change directories, and work with files, making you proficient in harnessing the true power of the terminal.

File Operations and Permissions

Understanding file operations and permissions is crucial for managing and securing your files effectively. In this part, we explore how to create, copy, move, and delete files and directories using various commands. Additionally, we delve into Linux file permissions, granting you the ability to control access to files and safeguard sensitive data.

Managing Processes and Services

Kali Linux runs numerous processes and services simultaneously to perform its functions. Here, we demystify the world of processes, teaching you how to view and manage running processes using commands. Furthermore, you'll learn how to control services, ensuring that your system operates efficiently and securely.

Working with Text Files

Text files are ubiquitous in the realm of Linux, and mastering their manipulation is indispensable. In this section, we explore powerful commands that enable you to view, search, and edit text files effortlessly. By the end of this part, you'll be equipped with the knowledge to handle configuration files, log files, and much more.

As we journey through the basic commands of Kali Linux, we lay the groundwork for the advanced cybersecurity techniques to come. Understanding the terminal is a stepping stone to becoming a proficient ethical hacker, allowing you to wield the full capabilities of this dynamic operating system.

So, let's roll up our sleeves and embrace the power of the command line. Together, we'll uncover the true potential of Kali Linux, setting the stage for the exciting chapters ahead.

Happy command-line exploring!

2.1 Navigating the Terminal

The terminal, also known as the command-line interface (CLI), is a powerful tool that allows users to interact with their computer using text-based commands. Navigating the terminal is a fundamental skill for any cybersecurity professional, as it provides a more efficient and flexible way to perform various tasks, such as file management, system configuration, and executing cybersecurity tools. In this section, we will explore the basic commands for navigating the terminal on a Linux system, including Kali Linux.

2.1.1 Accessing the Terminal

To access the terminal in Kali Linux, follow these steps:

Open a Terminal Emulator: By default, Kali Linux provides several terminal emulators, such as "Terminal," "Xfce Terminal," or "Konsole." You can find them in the application menu or by searching for "Terminal" in the search bar.

Launch the Terminal: Click on the terminal emulator icon to launch it. The terminal window will open, and you will see a text prompt that typically ends with a dollar sign ($) or a hash symbol (#).

Switch to Root User (Optional): Some administrative tasks require root privileges. To switch to the root user, use the su command followed by entering the root password when prompted. Keep in mind that administrative tasks should be performed with caution to avoid unintended consequences.

2.1.2 Basic Navigation Commands

Once you have accessed the terminal, you can use various commands to navigate the file system and execute commands. Here are some essential navigation commands:

pwd (Print Working Directory): This command displays the current working directory, which represents your current location in the file system.

ls (List): Use this command to list the contents of the current directory. By default, it shows only the names of files and directories in the current directory.

Options:

- -l: Long format, providing detailed information about files and directories.

- -a: Display hidden files (files whose names begin with a dot .).
- cd (Change Directory): This command allows you to change the current directory. To move to a specific directory, type cd followed by the directory path.

Example: cd /home/user/Documents

. (Current Directory) and .. (Parent Directory): These are special directory references. The single dot . represents the current directory, while the double dot .. represents the parent directory.

mkdir (Make Directory): Use this command to create a new directory.

Example: mkdir new_directory

rmdir (Remove Directory): Use this command to remove an empty directory.

Example: rmdir directory_to_remove

rm (Remove): This command allows you to remove files or directories.

Options:

- -r: Recursive, used to remove directories and their contents.

- -f: Force, bypassing confirmation prompts.

touch (Create Empty File): Use this command to create an empty file.

Example: touch new_file.txt

2.1.3 Wildcards

Wildcards are characters used to represent one or more characters in a file or directory name. They are helpful for performing actions on multiple files simultaneously. Here are some common wildcards:

* **(Asterisk):** Represents zero or more characters.

Example: ls *.txt lists all files with the .txt extension.

? (Question Mark): Represents a single character.

Example: ls file?.txt lists files like file1.txt, file2.txt, etc.

2.1.4 Using Tab Completion

Tab completion is a useful feature in the terminal that automatically completes commands, file names, and directory paths when you press the Tab key. This can save time and reduce the chance of typographical errors.

For example, if you want to change to the /home/user/Documents directory, you can type cd /home/u and then press the Tab key. The terminal will automatically complete the rest of the path, making it cd /home/user/.

2.1.5 Getting Help

If you need help with a specific command or want to learn more about its options and usage, you can use the man command to access the manual pages.

For example, to get information about the ls command, type man ls in the terminal and press Enter. The manual page will provide details on the command's usage, options, and examples.

2.1.6 Exiting the Terminal

To exit the terminal, you can use the exit command. Alternatively, you can press Ctrl + D to close the terminal window.

In conclusion, navigating the terminal is an essential skill for cybersecurity professionals, providing a text-based interface to interact with the file system and execute commands efficiently. Understanding basic navigation commands, using wildcards, and leveraging tab completion can significantly improve your productivity in the terminal and empower you to perform various cybersecurity tasks with confidence.

2.2 File Operations and Permissions

In the Linux terminal, file operations and permissions play a critical role in managing files and ensuring the security and integrity of data. As a cybersecurity professional, understanding how to work with files, directories, and their permissions is essential for effective system administration and data protection. In this section, we will explore common file operations, such as creating, copying, moving, and deleting files and directories, as well as managing file permissions.

2.2.1 Creating and Removing Files and Directories

To create a new file or directory, use the touch and mkdir commands, respectively:

touch (Create File): The touch command creates a new empty file or updates the timestamp of an existing file.

Example: touch new_file.txt

mkdir (Create Directory): The mkdir command creates a new directory (folder).

Example: mkdir new_directory

To remove files and directories, use the rm and rmdir commands:

rm (Remove): The rm command is used to delete files.

Example: rm unwanted_file.txt

To remove multiple files, use wildcards. For instance, rm *.txt removes all files with a .txt extension.

To remove directories and their contents, use the -r (recursive) option.

Example: rm -r unwanted_directory

rmdir (Remove Directory): The rmdir command is used to remove empty directories.

Example: rmdir empty_directory

To remove directories with contents, use rm -r instead.

2.2.2 Copying and Moving Files and Directories

To copy files and directories, use the cp command:

cp (Copy): The cp command copies files or directories from one location to another.

Example: cp source_file.txt destination_directory/

To copy directories and their contents, use the -r (recursive) option.

Example: cp -r source_directory/ destination_directory/

To move files and directories, use the mv command:

mv (Move): The mv command moves files or directories to a new location.

Example: mv file.txt new_location/

To rename files or directories, use mv and specify the new name.

Example: mv old_name.txt new_name.txt

2.2.3 File Permissions

In Linux, each file and directory has associated permissions that define who can read, write, and execute the file. Understanding and managing file permissions are crucial for ensuring data security and access control.

To view file permissions, use the ls command with the -l (long format) option:

Example: ls -l

The output will display file information, including permissions, owner, group, size, modification date, and filename.

File permissions are represented using a combination of letters and symbols:

- r (read): The file can be read if the letter is present (e.g., -r--r--r--).
- w (write): The file can be modified if the letter is present (e.g., --w--w--w-).
- x (execute): The file can be executed (e.g., -----x--x).

File permissions are categorized into three sets: user (owner), group, and others (everyone else). Each set has its own set of permissions, represented by three characters each:

- (dash): Indicates that a specific permission is not granted.

To modify file permissions, use the chmod command:

chmod (Change Mode): The chmod command is used to change file permissions.

Example: chmod +x script.sh adds execute permission to the file script.sh.

To set permissions explicitly, use numeric representation (octal):

- 4: Read permission (r)
- 2: Write permission (w)
- 1: Execute permission (x)

Example: chmod 755 file.txt sets read, write, and execute permissions for the owner, and read and execute permissions for the group and others.

2.2.4 Special Permissions

Some files may have special permissions, such as the set-user-ID (SUID), set-group-ID (SGID), and sticky bit.

SUID (Set-User-ID): When the SUID bit is set on an executable file, it allows the user executing the file to temporarily gain the privileges of the file's owner.

SGID (Set-Group-ID): When the SGID bit is set on an executable file or directory, it allows the user executing the file or creating new files in the directory to gain the group's privileges of the file or directory.

Sticky Bit: When the sticky bit is set on a directory, only the owner of a file within that directory can delete or rename the file.

To set special permissions, use the chmod command with numeric representation:

- SUID: chmod u+s file
- SGID: chmod g+s file
- Sticky Bit: chmod +t directory

In conclusion, understanding file operations and permissions is crucial for effective file management and data security in the Linux terminal. Being proficient in creating, copying, moving, and removing files and directories empowers cybersecurity professionals to efficiently organize and manipulate data. Moreover, mastering file permissions and special permissions ensures proper access control and data protection, strengthening the overall security of the system.

2.3 Managing Processes and Services

In the Linux operating system, processes and services are fundamental components that allow the system to execute tasks and provide various functionalities. As a cybersecurity professional, understanding how to manage processes and services is essential for monitoring system performance, troubleshooting issues, and ensuring the system's security. In this section, we will explore common commands and techniques for managing processes and services in a Linux environment, including Kali Linux.

2.3.1 Managing Processes

A process is a running instance of a program or command in the Linux system. Each process has a unique process ID (PID), and it can run in the background or foreground. Managing processes involves starting, stopping, monitoring, and controlling them.

ps (Process Status): The ps command displays information about currently running processes.

Example: ps aux displays a detailed list of all running processes, including those of other users.

The top command provides real-time dynamic information about running processes, system resource usage, and more. Press q to exit the top command.

kill (Terminate Process): The kill command terminates or sends a signal to a process.

Example: kill PID terminates the process with the specified PID.

To force the termination of a process, use kill -9 PID.

killall (Terminate by Name): The killall command terminates processes by their name.

Example: killall firefox terminates all processes named "firefox."

Foreground and Background Execution:

To run a process in the foreground, simply execute the command in the terminal.

To run a process in the background, add an ampersand & at the end of the command.

Example: ping example.com &

bg and fg (Background and Foreground): The bg and fg commands control background and foreground jobs, respectively.

Example: bg %1 sends a background job to run.

Example: fg %1 brings a background job to the foreground.

jobs (View Background Jobs): The jobs command displays a list of background jobs.

2.3.2 Managing Services

Services are background processes that provide specific functionalities to the system or network. In Linux, services are managed using a service manager, and the most common service manager is systemd.

systemctl (Control Systemd Services): The systemctl command is used to manage services in systemd.

Start a service: sudo systemctl start service_name

Stop a service: sudo systemctl stop service_name

Restart a service: sudo systemctl restart service_name

Enable a service to start at boot: sudo systemctl enable service_name

Disable a service from starting at boot: sudo systemctl disable service_name

View the status of a service: sudo systemctl status service_name

Example: sudo systemctl start apache2 starts the Apache web server.

journalctl (View Systemd Journal): The journalctl command allows you to view the system log, including service logs.

Example: sudo journalctl -u service_name displays the log of a specific service.
chkconfig (Manage SysVinit Services - Optional): Some older Linux systems use SysVinit as the service manager. On those systems, you can use chkconfig to manage services.

Start a service: sudo service service_name start

Stop a service: sudo service service_name stop

Restart a service: sudo service service_name restart

Enable a service to start at boot: sudo chkconfig service_name on

Disable a service from starting at boot: sudo chkconfig service_name off

Example: sudo service apache2 start starts the Apache web server.

2.3.3 Analyzing Resource Usage

Monitoring system resource usage is crucial for identifying performance issues and potential security threats.

top and htop: As mentioned earlier, top provides real-time information about running processes and system resource usage. htop is a more user-friendly alternative to top and offers additional features like mouse support and color-coded resource usage.

Install htop: If htop is not already installed, you can install it using your package manager.

Example (Debian-based systems): sudo apt update && sudo apt install htop

free (Memory Usage): The free command displays information about system memory usage.

Example: free -h displays memory usage in a human-readable format.

df (Disk Usage): The df command shows information about disk space usage.

Example: df -h displays disk usage in a human-readable format.

du (Disk Usage of Files and Directories): The du command estimates the disk usage of files and directories.

Example: du -sh /path/to/directory shows the total size of the directory in human-readable format.

In conclusion, managing processes and services is a critical skill for cybersecurity professionals to maintain system efficiency, identify potential issues, and secure the system. By understanding how to monitor and control processes, manage services, and analyze resource usage, you can ensure that your Linux system, including Kali Linux, functions optimally and remains secure.

2.4 Working with Text Files

Text files are a common data format used in Linux and are essential for various tasks, including scripting, configuration files, and log files. As a cybersecurity professional, mastering text file manipulation is crucial for analyzing log files, editing configurations, and processing data. In this section, we will explore common commands and techniques for working with text files in the Linux terminal, focusing on Kali Linux.

2.4.1 Viewing Text Files

To view the contents of a text file, you can use several commands in the terminal:

cat (Concatenate): The cat command displays the entire content of a text file.

Example: cat file.txt

less and more: These commands allow you to view the content of large text files page by page.

Example: less file.txt

Use the arrow keys to scroll, and press q to exit.

head and tail: These commands display the beginning or the end of a text file, respectively.

Example: head file.txt displays the first few lines of the file.

Example: tail file.txt displays the last few lines of the file.

The -n option can be used to specify the number of lines to display (e.g., tail -n 10 file.txt shows the last 10 lines).

2.4.2 Creating and Editing Text Files

To create or edit text files, you can use text editors or redirection:

Text Editors:

nano: Nano is a simple and user-friendly text editor available in most Linux distributions.

Example: nano new_file.txt opens nano to create or edit the file.

Press Ctrl + X to exit nano. If changes were made, you'll be prompted to save them.

vi and vim: Vi and Vim are powerful text editors with a steeper learning curve but offer advanced features and extensibility.

Example: vi new_file.txt opens vi to create or edit the file.

Press Esc, then :wq and Enter to save and exit vi.

Redirection:

> (Output Redirection): The > symbol redirects the output of a command to a file, creating or overwriting it.

Example: echo "Hello, World!" > greetings.txt creates a new file greetings.txt containing the text "Hello, World!"

>> (Append Redirection): The >> symbol appends the output of a command to a file, preserving existing content.

Example: echo "How are you?" >> greetings.txt appends the text "How are you?" to the existing greetings.txt file.

2.4.3 Searching Text in Files

To search for specific text patterns within a file, you can use the grep command:

grep: The grep command searches for text patterns in files.

Example: grep "error" logfile.txt searches for lines containing the word "error" in the logfile.txt file.

To search recursively in a directory and its subdirectories, use the -r option.

Example: grep -r "keyword" /path/to/directory

To perform a case-insensitive search, use the -i option.

Example: grep -i "warning" logfile.txt

2.4.4 Text File Manipulation

Various commands can help you manipulate text files:

cut: The cut command extracts specific columns from a text file based on a delimiter.

Example: cut -d ',' -f 1,3 data.csv extracts the first and third columns from a CSV file using the comma as the delimiter.

sort: The sort command sorts the lines of a text file alphabetically or numerically.

Example: sort file.txt sorts the lines of file.txt alphabetically.

To sort numerically, use the -n option.

Example: sort -n numbers.txt

uniq: The uniq command removes duplicate adjacent lines from a sorted file.

Example: uniq sorted.txt removes duplicate lines from the sorted.txt file.

To count the occurrences of each line, use the -c option.

Example: uniq -c sorted.txt

sed: Sed is a stream editor used for text transformation and editing.

Example: sed 's/old_text/new_text/g' file.txt replaces all occurrences of old_text with new_text in file.txt.

awk: Awk is a versatile text processing tool that can extract and manipulate data in text files.

Example: awk '{print $1}' data.txt prints the first column of the data.txt file.

In conclusion, working with text files is a fundamental skill for cybersecurity professionals, enabling them to analyze logs, edit configurations, and process data efficiently. By mastering commands for viewing, creating, editing, searching, and manipulating text files, you can become proficient in handling various text-based tasks in the Linux terminal, including Kali Linux.

Chapter 3: Information Gathering Techniques

Welcome to Chapter 3 of "The Kali Linux Handbook: A Practical Guide to Advanced Cybersecurity Techniques." In this chapter, we embark on a crucial phase of any cybersecurity assessment—the information gathering stage. Ethical hackers and security professionals rely on this critical phase to gain valuable insights into potential targets, identify vulnerabilities, and plan their approach strategically.

Passive Reconnaissance: Footprinting

In this section, we explore the art of passive reconnaissance, also known as footprinting. We'll learn how to gather valuable information about target systems and networks without directly interacting with them. By leveraging publicly available data and online resources, you'll uncover valuable details about the target's infrastructure, domain names, IP addresses, and more.

Active Reconnaissance: Scanning Networks

Taking our information gathering to the next level, active reconnaissance involves actively probing the target's systems and networks to gather additional data. We'll delve into network scanning techniques using various tools in Kali Linux, such as Nmap. You'll learn how to identify open ports, discover running services, and gain insights into the network's architecture.

Enumerating Hosts and Services

In this part, we take a deep dive into host and service enumeration. We'll build upon the information gathered in the previous sections to identify specific hosts and their associated services within the target network. Armed with this knowledge, you'll be better equipped to assess potential vulnerabilities and devise an effective penetration testing strategy.

Harvesting Data from Online Sources

The internet is a treasure trove of data, and skilled ethical hackers know how to harness it effectively. In this final section, we explore techniques for gathering data from web services, social media platforms, and other online sources. By combining open-source intelligence (OSINT) with our earlier findings, you'll be able to piece together a comprehensive profile of the target, laying the groundwork for successful cybersecurity assessments.

As we delve into the art of information gathering, remember that ethical hacking is about using these techniques responsibly and legally. The information you gather is instrumental in fortifying cybersecurity defenses and protecting organizations from potential threats.

By mastering information gathering techniques, you'll develop a sharper eye for reconnaissance, setting the stage for the upcoming chapters where we'll apply this knowledge to identify and address security vulnerabilities. So, let's sharpen our skills and uncover the secrets that lie hidden within the digital landscape.

Happy reconnaissance!

3.1 Passive Reconnaissance: Footprinting

Passive reconnaissance, also known as footprinting, is the initial phase of the cybersecurity reconnaissance process. During this phase, cybersecurity professionals gather information about a target system or organization without directly engaging with it. Footprinting involves collecting publicly available data from various sources to build a comprehensive understanding of the target's infrastructure, systems, and potential vulnerabilities. In this section, we will explore the methods and tools used for passive reconnaissance, highlighting the importance of ethical and legal considerations in the process.

3.1.1 Purpose of Footprinting

Footprinting serves as the foundation for any cybersecurity assessment or penetration testing activity. Its primary objectives include:

Information Gathering: Footprinting aims to obtain as much information as possible about the target system, organization, or individual. This information can include domain names, IP addresses, email addresses, employee names, technology in use, and more.

Identifying Attack Surfaces: By understanding the target's digital footprint, cybersecurity professionals can identify potential attack surfaces or entry points that could be exploited during an attack.

Assessing Security Posture: Footprinting helps assess the target's security posture by identifying potential weaknesses, such as publicly exposed sensitive information, outdated software, or misconfigured systems.

Risk Assessment: Through passive reconnaissance, cybersecurity professionals can identify potential risks and vulnerabilities that need to be addressed to strengthen the target's overall security.

3.1.2 Sources of Information for Footprinting

Passive reconnaissance relies on publicly available information from various sources, including:

Public Websites: Information from the target's official website, subdomains, and other web properties can provide valuable insights into the organization's products, services, and employees.

Search Engines: Search engines like Google can be used to discover information that may not be directly accessible through the target's website. Advanced search operators can narrow down search results to specific domains or file types.

Social Media: Social media platforms can reveal details about the organization's employees, partnerships, events, and activities.

Public Records and Registries: Public records, business directories, and domain registration information can provide details about the target's legal entity, ownership, and contact information.

Network Tools: Tools like WHOIS, DNS lookup, and IP geolocation services can help gather information about domain names, IP addresses, and network infrastructure.

Archive Websites: Websites that archive historical versions of web pages can provide insights into the target's past activities and changes in its online presence.

Job Postings and Career Pages: Job postings and career pages on the target's website can reveal technology stacks, software used, and potential skills of employees.

3.1.3 Ethical and Legal Considerations

While footprinting is a critical phase of reconnaissance, it is essential to perform these activities ethically and legally. Here are some ethical considerations to keep in mind:

Permission: Ensure you have permission to conduct footprinting activities. Unauthorized reconnaissance can be illegal and may lead to severe consequences.

Publicly Available Information: Limit your footprinting activities to publicly available information. Do not attempt to access restricted or private data.

Data Privacy: Respect data privacy regulations and avoid collecting sensitive or personally identifiable information without consent.

Responsible Disclosure: If you discover any security vulnerabilities or weaknesses during footprinting, follow responsible disclosure practices to report them to the target organization.

No Harm Principle: Do not engage in any activity that could cause harm to the target's systems or disrupt their operations.

3.1.4 Tools for Footprinting

Several tools can assist cybersecurity professionals in passive reconnaissance and footprinting:

Google Dorks: Google Dorks are advanced search queries used to find specific information on search engines.

WHOIS Lookup Tools: WHOIS tools provide domain registration information, including the domain owner's contact details.

DNS Lookup Tools: DNS lookup tools reveal domain-related information, such as DNS records and subdomains.

TheHarvester: TheHarvester is a tool for gathering email addresses, subdomains, and other information from various sources.

Shodan: Shodan is a search engine for discovering internet-connected devices, including open ports and services.

Maltego: Maltego is a data visualization tool that helps to gather and analyze information from various sources.

Social Media Platforms: Social media platforms themselves can be valuable sources of information during footprinting.

In conclusion, passive reconnaissance, or footprinting, is a crucial initial step in cybersecurity assessment and penetration testing. By gathering publicly available information about the target system or organization, cybersecurity professionals can gain valuable insights into potential vulnerabilities and attack surfaces. It is essential to conduct footprinting ethically, respecting legal boundaries and data privacy regulations. Using various tools and techniques, cybersecurity professionals can effectively perform passive reconnaissance to lay the groundwork for further assessment and security measures.

3.2 Active Reconnaissance: Scanning Networks

Active reconnaissance, also known as network scanning, is the second phase of the cybersecurity reconnaissance process. Unlike passive reconnaissance, active reconnaissance involves actively probing the target's network and systems to gather more detailed information about their structure, open ports, services, and potential vulnerabilities. In this section, we will explore the methods and tools used for network scanning during active reconnaissance, while emphasizing the need for ethical and controlled scanning to avoid any disruptive or harmful impact.

3.2.1 Purpose of Network Scanning

Network scanning serves as a proactive approach to gather detailed information about the target's network infrastructure. Its primary objectives include:

Network Mapping: Network scanning helps map the target's network by discovering devices, hosts, and their interconnections. This provides a comprehensive understanding of the target's network topology.

Port and Service Enumeration: Network scanning identifies open ports and services running on each network device. Understanding open ports is crucial for identifying potential entry points for exploitation.

Vulnerability Assessment: By identifying open ports and services, network scanning allows cybersecurity professionals to assess potential vulnerabilities and security weaknesses.

Asset Identification: Active reconnaissance helps identify all active assets on the target network, including servers, routers, switches, and other network devices.

Firewall and Security Policy Analysis: Scanning the network can provide insights into the effectiveness of firewall configurations and overall security policies.

3.2.2 Network Scanning Techniques

Various network scanning techniques are used during active reconnaissance:

Ping Sweeping: Ping sweeping is a basic technique that involves sending ICMP echo requests (ping) to a range of IP addresses to check which ones respond. Responding IP addresses indicate active hosts.

Port Scanning: Port scanning involves probing target hosts to identify open ports and services. Common port scanning techniques include:

TCP Connect Scan: Connects to target ports to check if they are open.

TCP SYN Scan (Half-Open Scan): Initiates a SYN packet to the target port and analyzes the response to determine if the port is open or closed.

TCP FIN Scan: Sends a FIN packet to the target port and analyzes the response. A lack of response indicates an open port.

TCP NULL, Xmas, and FIN Scan: Similar to the TCP FIN scan, these techniques exploit certain flag combinations in TCP packets to identify open ports.

Service Identification: Service identification involves determining the version and type of services running on open ports. Tools like Nmap can provide detailed service banners.

Operating System Identification: By analyzing the responses received during scanning, cybersecurity professionals can attempt to determine the operating system of the target hosts.

3.2.3 Ethical and Legal Considerations

Network scanning is an active and potentially intrusive activity, and conducting it ethically and responsibly is paramount. Some key considerations include:

Permission: Always obtain explicit permission from the target organization or system owner before conducting any network scanning.

Scope and Limitations: Clearly define the scope of the scanning activity and avoid scanning systems beyond the authorized scope.

Avoiding Disruptions: Use scanning techniques that are non-disruptive to the target's network and services. Avoid resource-intensive scans that could cause network or service degradation.

Data Privacy and Confidentiality: Be cautious not to access or disclose sensitive or confidential information during scanning.

Log Monitoring: If possible, coordinate with the target organization to monitor network logs and alert them about the scanning activity to avoid unnecessary alarms.

3.2.4 Tools for Network Scanning

Several tools are available to assist with network scanning during active reconnaissance:

Nmap: Nmap (Network Mapper) is a powerful and widely used open-source network scanning tool that supports various scanning techniques and service identification.

Zenmap: Zenmap is the graphical user interface (GUI) version of Nmap, providing a more user-friendly experience for network scanning.

Masscan: Masscan is a fast and asynchronous mass port scanner designed for large-scale network scanning.

hping3: hping3 is a versatile command-line tool for crafting and sending custom TCP/IP packets, useful for various scanning techniques.

Netcat (nc): Netcat is a versatile networking utility that can be used for port scanning and banner grabbing.

OpenVAS: OpenVAS (Open Vulnerability Assessment System) is an open-source vulnerability scanner that can be used for in-depth vulnerability assessment.

In conclusion, active reconnaissance through network scanning is a critical phase in cybersecurity assessment and penetration testing. By actively probing the target's network and systems, cybersecurity professionals can gain valuable insights into the network topology, open ports, and services, leading to a better understanding of potential vulnerabilities. However, it is essential to conduct network scanning ethically, with proper authorization and controlled techniques to avoid any disruptions or negative impacts on the target's network.

3.3 Enumerating Hosts and Services

During the active reconnaissance phase of cybersecurity assessment, enumerating hosts and services is a critical step to gain a deeper understanding of the target network's infrastructure.

Enumeration involves actively probing and systematically gathering information about hosts, devices, and the services running on them. This process helps cybersecurity professionals identify potential attack vectors, vulnerabilities, and misconfigurations that could be exploited during an attack. In this section, we will explore the methods and tools used for enumerating hosts and services, while emphasizing the importance of conducting these activities responsibly and ethically.

3.3.1 Purpose of Host and Service Enumeration

Host and service enumeration serve as crucial components of active reconnaissance, with specific objectives, including:

Host Discovery: The primary objective of host enumeration is to discover all active hosts within the target network. This process involves identifying live systems and their IP addresses.

Port and Service Enumeration: By probing each host, cybersecurity professionals can enumerate the open ports and services running on those ports. This information provides insights into potential entry points and attack surfaces.

Banner Grabbing: Banner grabbing is the process of capturing service banners or information sent by services upon connection. This helps identify the version and type of running services, aiding in vulnerability assessment.

Operating System Identification: By analyzing the responses from hosts, cybersecurity professionals can attempt to determine the operating system (OS) running on each host. OS identification is essential for tailoring specific attacks to the target system.

User Enumeration: In some cases, enumeration may also involve gathering information about valid user accounts or resources accessible on the network.

3.3.2 Methods for Host and Service Enumeration

Several methods are used for host and service enumeration during active reconnaissance:

Ping Sweeping: Ping sweeping, which is also used in network scanning, involves sending ICMP echo requests (ping) to a range of IP addresses to identify live hosts that respond.

TCP Port Scanning: TCP port scanning techniques, such as TCP connect scan, TCP SYN scan, and others (mentioned in the previous section), are used to identify open ports on hosts.

UDP Port Scanning: UDP port scanning involves sending UDP packets to identify open UDP ports on hosts. UDP scanning can be more challenging than

TCP scanning due to the connectionless nature of UDP.

Banner Grabbing: Banner grabbing involves connecting to open ports and capturing the service banners or response messages from the services running on those ports.

OS Fingerprinting: OS fingerprinting techniques, such as TCP/IP stack fingerprinting or passive OS fingerprinting, attempt to determine the operating system of the target hosts based on their responses to certain probes.

User Enumeration: In the context of network services, user enumeration refers to the process of identifying valid user accounts or resources accessible on the network. This is often encountered in authentication systems.

3.3.3 Ethical and Legal Considerations

Host and service enumeration are active activities that involve interacting with the target's network. To ensure ethical and responsible enumeration:

Permission: Always obtain explicit permission from the target organization or system owner before conducting any host and service enumeration.

Scope and Limitations: Clearly define the scope of the enumeration activity and avoid probing systems beyond the authorized scope.

Minimize Impact: Use enumeration techniques that are non-disruptive to the target's network and services. Avoid resource-intensive scans that could cause network or service degradation.

Data Privacy and Confidentiality: Be cautious not to access or disclose sensitive or confidential information during enumeration.

Responsible Disclosure: If you discover any vulnerabilities or weaknesses during enumeration, follow responsible disclosure practices to report them to the target organization.

3.3.4 Tools for Host and Service Enumeration

Several tools assist cybersecurity professionals in host and service enumeration during active reconnaissance:

Nmap: Nmap (Network Mapper) is a versatile open-source tool that supports various host and service enumeration techniques, including port scanning, banner grabbing, and OS fingerprinting.

Hping3: Hping3 is a powerful command-line tool for crafting and sending custom TCP/IP packets, useful for various enumeration tasks.

Netcat (nc): Netcat can be used for banner grabbing and testing port connectivity.

OpenVAS: OpenVAS is an open-source vulnerability scanner that can perform host and service enumeration as part of its vulnerability assessment capabilities.

BannerGrab: BannerGrab is a tool designed specifically for banner grabbing and extracting service information from open ports.

In conclusion, host and service enumeration is a critical phase of active reconnaissance in cybersecurity assessments. By systematically gathering information about live hosts, open ports, and running services, cybersecurity professionals can identify potential vulnerabilities and attack vectors. However, it is essential to conduct host and service enumeration ethically and responsibly, with proper authorization and controlled techniques, to avoid any disruptions or negative impacts on the target's network.

3.4 Harvesting Data from Online Sources

Harvesting data from online sources is a vital aspect of active reconnaissance in cybersecurity assessments. It involves gathering information from publicly available online platforms and sources to gain insights into the target's digital footprint, potential vulnerabilities, and other relevant details. While this data collection can aid cybersecurity professionals in understanding the target's online presence, it is essential to conduct data harvesting responsibly, ethically, and in compliance with data privacy regulations. In this section, we will explore the methods and tools used for data harvesting from online sources.

3.4.1 Purpose of Data Harvesting

The primary purpose of data harvesting from online sources is to obtain valuable information about the target, which can include:

Domain and Subdomain Enumeration: Harvesting data allows cybersecurity professionals to identify the target's primary domain and any associated subdomains.

Email Addresses and Contact Information: Gathering data can reveal email addresses, contact details, and other means of communication used by the target organization or individuals.

Publicly Accessible Files: Data harvesting can uncover publicly accessible files, directories, and documents hosted on the target's web servers. These files may contain sensitive information unintentionally exposed to the public.

Software and Technology Stack Identification: Harvesting data from online sources may reveal the technologies and software used by the target, helping to assess potential vulnerabilities associated with those technologies.

Employee Information: Publicly available employee profiles on social media and professional networking sites may provide insights into the target's workforce and potential points of contact.

3.4.2 Methods for Data Harvesting

Data harvesting from online sources involves various methods and techniques:

Search Engines: Utilizing search engines like Google, Bing, or Shodan, cybersecurity professionals can use advanced search queries (Google Dorks) to discover specific information about the target.

Web Scraping: Web scraping involves automated extraction of data from websites. Custom scripts or tools can be used to crawl web pages and collect relevant information.

Social Media Mining: Cybersecurity professionals can mine social media platforms for publicly available information, such as employee details, partner relationships, events, and more.

Public APIs: Some online platforms offer public APIs that allow access to non-sensitive data. Cybersecurity professionals can use these APIs to retrieve information relevant to their assessment.

DNS Enumeration: Enumerating DNS records can reveal domain names, subdomains, and associated IP addresses.

Certificate Transparency Logs: Certificate transparency logs provide information about SSL/TLS certificates issued for domains, which can help identify additional subdomains.

3.4.3 Ethical and Legal Considerations

Data harvesting, even when limited to publicly available sources, must be conducted ethically and responsibly:

Permission: Obtain explicit permission from the target organization or system owner before conducting any data harvesting activities.

Data Privacy and Compliance: Be mindful of data privacy regulations and avoid collecting sensitive or personally identifiable information without consent.

Responsible Use: Use the harvested data only for the purpose of the cybersecurity assessment and avoid any unauthorized or harmful use.

Publicly Available Information: Limit data harvesting to publicly accessible information and refrain from attempting to access restricted or private data.

Terms of Service and Robots.txt: Adhere to the website's terms of service and respect the rules specified in the robots.txt file, if available.

3.4.4 Tools for Data Harvesting

Various tools and techniques can assist cybersecurity professionals in data harvesting from online sources:

Google Dorks: Google Dorks are advanced search queries used to discover specific information on Google.

Shodan: Shodan is a search engine for internet-connected devices and services, providing valuable information for cybersecurity assessments.

Web Scraping Libraries: Python libraries like BeautifulSoup and Scrapy enable web scraping to extract data from websites.

Social Media APIs: APIs provided by social media platforms can be used to collect publicly available data from their platforms.

Subdomain Enumeration Tools: Tools like Sublist3r, Knock, and others can assist in enumerating subdomains.

Certificate Transparency Logs: Certificate transparency logs can be accessed directly or through tools like crt.sh to search for SSL/TLS certificates associated with domains.

In conclusion, data harvesting from online sources is a critical phase of active reconnaissance in cybersecurity assessments. By gathering publicly available information, cybersecurity professionals can gain valuable insights into the target's digital footprint, potential vulnerabilities, and relevant details. To ensure responsible and ethical data harvesting, explicit permission must be obtained, data privacy regulations must be adhered to, and any unauthorized or harmful use of the harvested data must be avoided.

Chapter 4: Vulnerability Assessment and Exploitation

Welcome to Chapter 4 of "The Kali Linux Handbook: A Practical Guide to Advanced Cybersecurity Techniques." In this crucial chapter, we venture into the heart of ethical hacking—vulnerability assessment and exploitation. Armed with the information gathered from the previous chapters, we'll learn how to identify and exploit weaknesses within the target's systems, simulating real-world cyberattacks to strengthen security defenses.

Identifying System Vulnerabilities

In this section, we dive deep into the process of vulnerability assessment. You'll learn how to use powerful tools in Kali Linux to scan for potential weaknesses in the target's systems and applications. By understanding common vulnerabilities such as outdated software, misconfigurations, and weak authentication mechanisms, you'll be better equipped to identify potential entry points for exploitation.

Exploiting Software Vulnerabilities

Having identified vulnerabilities, it's time to explore the art of exploitation. In this part, we'll explore techniques for leveraging security flaws in software and services to gain unauthorized access. Through hands-on examples and step-by-step guidance, you'll understand how attackers exploit weaknesses and how ethical hackers can use the same techniques to fortify defenses.

Using Metasploit Framework

The Metasploit Framework is a powerful tool that deserves its own dedicated section. In this part, we delve into the world of Metasploit, a versatile penetration testing platform that simplifies vulnerability exploitation. You'll learn how to use Metasploit's vast array of modules to automate the process of identifying, validating, and exploiting vulnerabilities in a target system.

Post-Exploitation Techniques

Once a system is compromised, the battle is far from over. In this final section, we explore post-exploitation techniques, essential for maintaining access and pivoting within the target's environment. From escalating privileges to covering tracks, you'll gain the knowledge needed to maneuver stealthily and effectively after successful exploitation.

Throughout this chapter, we stress the ethical use of vulnerability assessment and exploitation techniques. The goal is to understand and defend against potential threats, rather than causing harm. By walking in the footsteps of ethical hackers, you'll cultivate a deeper appreciation for proactive cybersecurity measures.

As we progress through vulnerability assessment and exploitation, we prepare ourselves for the challenges that lie ahead. Armed with knowledge and expertise, we are better equipped to safeguard against cyber threats, making the digital world a safer place for everyone.

Let's embrace the responsibilities of ethical hacking and delve into the realm of vulnerability assessment and exploitation.

4.1 Identifying System Vulnerabilities

Identifying system vulnerabilities is a crucial aspect of cybersecurity assessment and penetration testing. Vulnerabilities are weaknesses or flaws in a system's design, configuration, or implementation that can be exploited by malicious actors to gain unauthorized access, disrupt services, or steal sensitive information. In this section, we will explore the methods and tools used to identify system vulnerabilities, the importance of vulnerability databases, and the significance of responsible disclosure.

4.1.1 Methods for Identifying Vulnerabilities

There are several methods used to identify system vulnerabilities during cybersecurity assessments:

Vulnerability Scanning: Vulnerability scanning involves using automated tools to scan the target system or network for known vulnerabilities. These tools compare the system's configuration and software versions against a database of known vulnerabilities to identify potential weaknesses.

Manual Assessment: Manual assessment involves in-depth analysis by cybersecurity professionals to identify vulnerabilities that automated tools might miss. This process requires a deep understanding of system architecture and security best practices.

Penetration Testing: Penetration testing, also known as ethical hacking, involves simulating real-world attacks on the target system to discover vulnerabilities. Penetration testers use a combination of automated tools and manual techniques to exploit weaknesses and gain unauthorized access.

Code Review: In the case of software applications, code review involves examining the source code to identify programming errors or security vulnerabilities.

Fuzz Testing: Fuzz testing involves sending random or unexpected inputs to a system to uncover vulnerabilities related to input handling and error handling.

Security Auditing: Security auditing involves reviewing the system's security policies, configurations, and access controls to identify misconfigurations or weak security settings.

4.1.2 Tools for Identifying Vulnerabilities

Various tools can assist in identifying system vulnerabilities:

Nessus: Nessus is a popular vulnerability scanner that can perform automated scans to identify known vulnerabilities in systems and networks.

OpenVAS: OpenVAS is an open-source vulnerability scanner that provides similar functionality to Nessus.

Nmap: Nmap, besides network scanning, can also be used to identify open ports and services, which may reveal potential vulnerabilities.

Metasploit: Metasploit is a penetration testing framework that includes numerous exploit modules to test for vulnerabilities.

Burp Suite: Burp Suite is a web application security testing tool that can be used for web vulnerability scanning and manual testing.

4.1.3 Vulnerability Databases

Vulnerability databases play a crucial role in identifying system vulnerabilities. These databases maintain a comprehensive list of known vulnerabilities and their associated details, including severity, impact, and recommended mitigations. Some well-known vulnerability databases include:

National Vulnerability Database (NVD): NVD, managed by the National Institute of Standards and Technology (NIST), is the U.S. government repository of standardized vulnerability information.

Common Vulnerabilities and Exposures (CVE): CVE is a list of common names for publicly known cybersecurity vulnerabilities and exposures, maintained by the MITRE Corporation.

Exploit Database (Exploit-DB): Exploit-DB is a non-profit project that provides a collection of exploits and vulnerability information.

4.1.4 Responsible Disclosure

Once vulnerabilities are identified, responsible disclosure is essential. Responsible disclosure involves reporting the discovered vulnerabilities to the affected vendors or organizations so they can take appropriate action to patch or mitigate the vulnerabilities. Key considerations for responsible disclosure include:

Notify the Vendor: Contact the vendor or organization that owns the system affected by the vulnerability and provide detailed information about the vulnerability.

Give Adequate Time: Allow the vendor sufficient time to develop and release a patch before disclosing the vulnerability publicly.

Coordination with CERTs: In some cases, coordinating with Computer Emergency Response Teams (CERTs) or cybersecurity authorities can facilitate responsible disclosure.

Public Disclosure: If the vendor fails to address the vulnerability within a reasonable time frame, responsible disclosure may involve publicly disclosing the vulnerability to raise awareness and prompt action.

Bug Bounty Programs: Some organizations offer bug bounty programs, where ethical hackers are rewarded for responsibly disclosing vulnerabilities.

In conclusion, identifying system vulnerabilities is a critical step in cybersecurity assessments to assess the system's security posture and address potential weaknesses. Various methods, including vulnerability scanning, manual assessment, penetration testing, and code review, are used to identify vulnerabilities.

Vulnerability databases play a vital role in cataloging known vulnerabilities, and responsible disclosure is essential to ensure that vulnerabilities are addressed in a timely and appropriate manner.

4.2 Exploiting Software Vulnerabilities

Exploiting software vulnerabilities is a key aspect of penetration testing and ethical hacking. While the primary goal of penetration testing is to identify and remediate vulnerabilities, ethical hackers may need to demonstrate the impact of these vulnerabilities to raise awareness and prompt action from system owners. In this section, we will explore the process of exploiting software vulnerabilities, the importance of responsible and controlled testing, and the ethical considerations involved in this practice.

4.2.1 Understanding Software Vulnerabilities

Software vulnerabilities are weaknesses or flaws in software applications or systems that can be exploited to compromise their security. Common types of software vulnerabilities include:

Buffer Overflows: Buffer overflows occur when a program writes more data to a buffer (temporary storage) than it can hold, leading to data corruption and potential code execution.

SQL Injection: SQL injection occurs when an attacker inserts malicious SQL code into an application's input fields, allowing unauthorized access to a database.

Cross-Site Scripting (XSS): XSS vulnerabilities enable attackers to inject malicious scripts into web pages viewed by other users, potentially stealing their information or hijacking their sessions.

Remote Code Execution (RCE): RCE vulnerabilities allow attackers to execute code remotely on a system, gaining complete control over it.

Authentication Bypass: Authentication bypass vulnerabilities enable attackers to gain access to a system without proper credentials.

Privilege Escalation: Privilege escalation vulnerabilities allow attackers to elevate their privileges to gain more control over a system.

4.2.2 Process of Exploiting Software Vulnerabilities

The process of exploiting software vulnerabilities typically involves the following steps:

Discovery: Ethical hackers first identify potential vulnerabilities through vulnerability scanning, manual assessment, or penetration testing.

Research and Analysis: Hackers analyze the discovered vulnerabilities to understand their nature, potential impact, and possible exploitation techniques.

Proof of Concept (PoC): Ethical hackers develop PoCs to demonstrate the successful exploitation of the vulnerabilities. PoCs show how the vulnerability can be leveraged to compromise the system.

Exploitation: Once the PoCs are ready, ethical hackers execute the exploitation process to demonstrate the impact of the vulnerabilities. This may involve gaining unauthorized access, executing arbitrary code, or accessing sensitive information.

Documentation: Detailed documentation of the exploitation process, including the steps taken and the results obtained, is prepared for further analysis and reporting.

4.2.3 Responsible and Controlled Testing

Exploiting software vulnerabilities should always be conducted responsibly and under controlled conditions:

Permission: Ensure that you have explicit permission from the system owner or organization before attempting to exploit vulnerabilities. Unauthorized exploitation is illegal and unethical.

Isolated Environment: Conduct all exploitation activities in a controlled and isolated testing environment. Avoid testing on production systems or systems not designated for testing purposes.

Limit Scope: Clearly define the scope of exploitation activities to stay within the authorized boundaries. Focus only on the agreed-upon targets and refrain from going beyond the specified scope.

Mitigation Measures: Apply appropriate mitigation measures to prevent unintended impacts on the target system. For example, disable automated blocking mechanisms, if possible, to avoid locking out legitimate users.

Monitoring and Control: Continuously monitor the exploitation process and have mechanisms in place to stop the test immediately if any unforeseen consequences arise.

4.2.4 Ethical Considerations

When exploiting software vulnerabilities, ethical hackers must adhere to strict ethical guidelines:

Intent: The primary intent of exploitation should be to demonstrate vulnerabilities and promote improved security, not to cause harm or damage.

Responsible Disclosure: After successful exploitation, promptly report the findings to the system owner or organization, along with recommendations for remediation.

Confidentiality: Treat all sensitive information obtained during exploitation with the utmost confidentiality and ensure it is not disclosed to unauthorized parties.

No Harm Principle: Do not engage in any activity that could cause harm, disruption, or unauthorized access beyond the scope of the penetration test.

Professionalism: Conduct exploitation activities with professionalism and adhere to industry best practices and ethical standards.

In conclusion, exploiting software vulnerabilities is a crucial aspect of penetration testing to demonstrate the impact of vulnerabilities and prompt necessary security improvements. However, ethical hackers must exercise great responsibility, adhere to strict ethical guidelines, and always seek explicit permission before attempting any exploitation. By conducting responsible and controlled testing, ethical hackers can play a vital role in enhancing overall system security and mitigating potential risks.

4.3 Using Metasploit Framework

The Metasploit Framework is a powerful open-source penetration testing tool used by ethical hackers and security professionals to identify, exploit, and validate vulnerabilities in systems. Developed by Rapid7, the Metasploit Framework simplifies the process of conducting penetration tests and provides a wide range of exploitation modules, payloads, and auxiliary tools. In this section, we will explore the basic concepts of using the Metasploit Framework and how it aids in penetration testing.

4.3.1 Key Components of Metasploit Framework

The Metasploit Framework consists of several key components:

Console Interface: The Metasploit console is the main user interface for interacting with the Framework. It allows users to execute commands, load modules, and manage sessions.

Exploit Modules: Exploit modules are pre-built code components that target specific vulnerabilities in various software applications. These modules are designed to exploit known weaknesses and gain unauthorized access to a system.

Payloads: Payloads are pieces of code that run on the exploited system after a successful penetration. They provide various functionalities, such as command execution, shell access, and meterpreter sessions, allowing the tester to interact with the compromised system.

Auxiliary Modules: Auxiliary modules are tools that perform specific tasks during a penetration test, such as port scanning, fingerprinting, or gathering information about the target.

Post-Exploitation Modules: Post-exploitation modules are used after successful exploitation to gather additional information, escalate privileges, or pivot to other systems on the network.

4.3.2 Using the Metasploit Console

To use the Metasploit Framework, you typically start by launching the Metasploit console. The console can be accessed through the command-line interface (CLI) or via the graphical user interface (GUI). Once the console is up and running, you can execute various commands and interact with the Framework.

Here are some common commands used in the Metasploit console:

- **use**: Selects a specific module for use, such as an exploit module or auxiliary module.
- **show**: Displays information about available modules, payloads, options, and sessions.
- **search**: Searches for modules based on specific criteria, such as a vulnerability name or keyword.
- **set**: Sets options and parameters for the selected module.
- **exploit**: Initiates the exploitation process using the selected module.
- **sessions**: Lists all active sessions established during the exploitation.

4.3.3 Conducting a Basic Exploitation

To conduct a basic exploitation using the Metasploit Framework, follow these steps:

Selecting the Exploit Module: Use the "use" command to select a specific exploit module that targets a known vulnerability in the target system.

Setting Options: Use the "show options" command to view the required options for the selected module. Set the necessary options with the "set" command, such as the target IP address and port.

Selecting the Payload: Use the "show payloads" command to view available payloads that can be used after successful exploitation. Select a payload that suits your objectives.

Setting Payload Options: Similar to the exploit module, use the "show options" and "set" commands to configure the payload with any required options.

Exploiting the Vulnerability: Once the exploit module and payload are configured, use the "exploit" command to attempt the exploitation.

Interacting with the Compromised System: If the exploitation is successful, you can interact with the compromised system through a meterpreter session or other available means.

4.3.4 Ethical and Responsible Use

It is crucial to use the Metasploit Framework ethically and responsibly:

Permission: Always obtain explicit permission from the system owner or organization before using Metasploit to conduct penetration tests.

Scope Limitation: Ensure that all exploitation activities are limited to the agreed-upon scope of the penetration test.

Data Privacy: Respect data privacy regulations and avoid accessing or disclosing sensitive or confidential information without proper authorization.

No Harm Principle: Do not engage in any activity that could cause harm, disruption, or unauthorized access beyond the scope of the penetration test.

Documentation: Maintain detailed documentation of all activities, findings, and exploitation results for reporting and analysis purposes.

In conclusion, the Metasploit Framework is a valuable tool for conducting penetration tests and demonstrating the impact of vulnerabilities in systems. By using Metasploit responsibly and ethically, security professionals can identify potential weaknesses, assist in remediation efforts, and enhance overall system security.

4.4 Post-Exploitation Techniques

Post-exploitation is a crucial phase of penetration testing and ethical hacking that occurs after an attacker successfully compromises a system. During this phase, ethical hackers seek to maintain and expand their access while gathering valuable information from the compromised system. The objective is to simulate real-world scenarios and assess the potential risks and impacts of a successful cyber-attack. In this section, we will explore some common post-exploitation techniques and their significance in cybersecurity assessments.

4.4.1 Objectives of Post-Exploitation

The primary objectives of post-exploitation techniques are as follows:

Persistence: Achieve persistence on the compromised system to ensure that the attacker can regain access even after system reboots or security measures are applied.

Privilege Escalation: Attempt to escalate privileges on the compromised system to gain higher levels of access, enabling more control over the system.

Lateral Movement: Explore the network and attempt to move laterally to other systems to expand the attacker's reach within the network.

Data Gathering: Collect valuable information from the compromised system, such as user credentials, sensitive files, or network configurations.

Covering Tracks: Erase or manipulate logs and other traces of the attacker's presence to remain undetected.

4.4.2 Common Post-Exploitation Techniques

Some common post-exploitation techniques used by ethical hackers include:

File System Navigation: Explore the file system to identify important files, configuration files, and sensitive data.

Privilege Escalation Exploits: Search for potential privilege escalation vulnerabilities that could grant higher levels of access on the system.

Process Enumeration: Enumerate running processes to identify valuable services or applications running on the system.

Service Enumeration: Identify services running on the compromised system and gather information about these services.

Credential Harvesting: Extract usernames, passwords, and other credentials stored on the system.

Pass-the-Hash: Use stolen password hashes to gain unauthorized access to other systems, without needing to know the actual passwords.

Keylogging: Install keyloggers to capture keystrokes made by users, potentially capturing sensitive information, such as login credentials.

Remote Desktop Protocol (RDP) Sessions: Hijack active RDP sessions to access remote desktops.

Network Scanning: Scan the local network to identify other vulnerable systems and expand the attack surface.

Data Exfiltration: Transfer sensitive data from the compromised system to the attacker's machine.

4.4.3 Ethical Considerations

Post-exploitation techniques carry significant ethical considerations, as they involve operating within a compromised system:

Permission: Always obtain explicit permission from the system owner or organization before conducting any post-exploitation activities.

Scope Limitation: Ensure that all post-exploitation activities are confined to the authorized scope of the penetration test.

Data Privacy: Respect data privacy regulations and avoid accessing or disclosing sensitive or confidential information without proper authorization.

Responsible Use: Exercise extreme caution to avoid any disruption or damage to the target system or network during post-exploitation.

Covering Tracks: Avoid making changes that could alert the system administrators to the presence of the attacker.

4.4.4 Post-Exploitation Tools

Several tools and frameworks are commonly used for post-exploitation activities:

Metasploit Framework: Metasploit provides a variety of post-exploitation modules and payloads for maintaining access, privilege escalation, and data exfiltration.

PowerShell Empire: PowerShell Empire is a post-exploitation framework that allows attackers to use PowerShell scripts to perform various activities on the compromised system.

Mimikatz: Mimikatz is a popular tool for harvesting credentials and performing privilege escalation on Windows systems.

Netcat (nc): Netcat can be used for various post-exploitation activities, including file transfer and remote shell access.

PsExec: PsExec is a Windows utility used to execute processes remotely on other systems.

In conclusion, post-exploitation techniques play a critical role in cybersecurity assessments to simulate real-world scenarios and assess the potential impact of successful cyber-attacks. By using these techniques responsibly and ethically, ethical hackers can assist in identifying potential risks, enhancing system security, and preparing organizations to defend against sophisticated cyber threats.

Chapter 5: Wireless Network Penetration Testing

Welcome to Chapter 5 of "The Kali Linux Handbook: A Practical Guide to Advanced Cybersecurity Techniques." In this chapter, we delve into the fascinating world of wireless network penetration testing—a critical skill for assessing and securing wireless networks in today's connected world.

Wireless Security Concepts

We begin with a comprehensive overview of wireless security concepts, exploring the different encryption protocols, authentication mechanisms, and security vulnerabilities commonly found in wireless networks. Understanding these fundamentals is essential before we proceed to explore the tools and techniques used to assess and secure wireless environments effectively.

Cracking WEP Encryption

In this section, we venture into the realm of cracking WEP (Wired Equivalent Privacy) encryption. Despite its weaknesses, WEP is still present in some legacy systems, making it an important topic to understand. You'll learn about the vulnerabilities in WEP and how to exploit them using Kali Linux tools to gain unauthorized access.

Attacking WPA/WPA2 Encryption

WPA (Wi-Fi Protected Access) and WPA2 are the more modern and robust encryption standards used in wireless networks. In this part, we explore the techniques to attack WPA/WPA2 encryption, such as dictionary attacks and brute-force methods. By the end of this section, you'll be proficient in cracking WPA/WPA2 passwords and understanding the importance of strong network security.

Wireless MITM Attacks

Man-in-the-Middle (MITM) attacks are powerful and dangerous techniques that allow attackers to intercept and manipulate data between connected devices. In this final section, we learn how to execute wireless MITM attacks using Kali Linux tools. You'll understand the significance of securing wireless communications to prevent these types of attacks and protect sensitive information.

As we venture into wireless network penetration testing, we emphasize the importance of ethical hacking and responsible use of these techniques. Conducting wireless assessments provides valuable insights into the security posture of wireless networks, enabling organizations to fortify their defenses against potential threats.

By mastering the art of wireless network penetration testing, you'll have the power to identify and address vulnerabilities that could be exploited by malicious actors. Let's embark on this journey to secure wireless environments and make the digital world safer for all.

Happy wireless penetration testing!

5.1 Wireless Security Concepts

Wireless networks have become an integral part of our daily lives, providing convenience and flexibility for connecting to the internet and other devices. However, their wireless nature also introduces unique security challenges that must be addressed to protect sensitive data and ensure the integrity of the network. In this section, we will explore key wireless security concepts and the measures taken to safeguard wireless networks from various threats.

5.1.1 Wireless Network Types

Wireless networks can be broadly categorized into two main types:

Wi-Fi (Wireless Fidelity) Networks: Wi-Fi networks use radio waves to provide wireless connectivity to devices such as laptops, smartphones, and tablets.

They are the most common type of wireless networks found in homes, businesses, and public places.

Cellular Networks: Cellular networks use mobile communication infrastructure to provide wireless connectivity to mobile devices. These networks are used for mobile data and voice communication and are operated by mobile service providers.

5.1.2 Wireless Security Threats

Wireless networks are susceptible to various security threats due to their open nature and the broadcast of radio signals. Some common wireless security threats include:

Eavesdropping (Sniffing): Attackers can intercept wireless traffic to capture sensitive information, such as passwords and private communications.

Unauthorized Access (Rogue Devices): Unauthorized users may connect rogue devices to the wireless network, gaining access to resources or compromising the network's security.

Denial of Service (DoS) Attacks: Attackers can flood the wireless network with excessive traffic, causing it to become unavailable to legitimate users.

Man-in-the-Middle (MitM) Attacks: In MitM attacks, attackers position themselves between the wireless client and the access point, intercepting and possibly altering data transmissions.

Evil Twin Attacks: In an evil twin attack, attackers set up a rogue wireless access point with a similar name to a legitimate network, tricking users into connecting to it.

Password Cracking: Weak or poorly configured wireless network security settings can be susceptible to password cracking attacks.

5.1.3 Wireless Security Measures

To mitigate the security risks associated with wireless networks, several security measures are implemented:

Encryption: Data transmitted over wireless networks is encrypted to prevent eavesdropping and unauthorized access. WPA2 (Wi-Fi Protected Access 2) and WPA3 are commonly used encryption protocols for Wi-Fi networks.

Secure Authentication: Strong authentication mechanisms, such as WPA2-Enterprise (802.1X) with EAP (Extensible Authentication Protocol), are used to ensure only authorized users can connect to the network.

Network Segmentation: Segmenting the wireless network from the wired network can minimize the impact of a successful breach.

Wireless Intrusion Detection/Prevention Systems (WIDS/WIPS): WIDS/WIPS continuously monitor wireless traffic for suspicious activities and unauthorized devices.

MAC Address Filtering: MAC address filtering allows only specific devices with pre-approved MAC addresses to connect to the network.

Disable SSID Broadcast: Disabling the broadcast of the network's SSID (Service Set Identifier) can make it less visible to casual attackers.

Regular Patching and Updates: Keeping wireless access points and devices up to date with the latest firmware and security patches helps protect against known vulnerabilities.

Strong Passwords and Passphrases: Enforcing strong and unique passwords or passphrases for Wi-Fi network access enhances security.

Use of Virtual Private Networks (VPNs): VPNs can be used to secure wireless connections, encrypting all data transmitted between the device and the VPN server.

5.1.4 Responsible Wireless Usage

In addition to technical security measures, responsible wireless usage is essential for maintaining security:

Public Wi-Fi Use: Exercise caution when using public Wi-Fi networks, as they are often less secure and more susceptible to attacks.

Bluetooth Security: Secure Bluetooth connections with strong passkeys and turn off Bluetooth when not in use.

Disable Unused Services: Disable any unused wireless services or features on devices to reduce the attack surface.

Physical Security: Physically secure wireless access points and routers to prevent unauthorized access.

In conclusion, wireless security concepts are vital for safeguarding wireless networks from a variety of threats. By implementing strong encryption, secure authentication, and other security measures, combined with responsible wireless usage, individuals and organizations can protect their wireless networks and data from potential security breaches.

5.2 Cracking WEP Encryption

Wired Equivalent Privacy (WEP) was the first encryption protocol used to secure Wi-Fi networks. However, due to its weaknesses and vulnerabilities, it is no longer considered secure and has been replaced by more robust encryption standards like WPA2 and WPA3. Despite its obsolescence, understanding the process of cracking WEP encryption can provide insights into the importance of using stronger security measures. In this section, we will explore the vulnerabilities of WEP encryption and the steps involved in cracking it.

5.2.1 Vulnerabilities of WEP Encryption

WEP encryption suffers from several fundamental vulnerabilities that render it easily crackable:

Weak Key Generation: WEP uses a 24-bit Initialization Vector (IV) to generate encryption keys, which results in a limited number of possible keys. This limitation makes it susceptible to brute-force attacks.

Static Key: WEP relies on a static encryption key that remains constant unless manually changed. This lack of key rotation makes it easier for attackers to collect enough data to launch an attack.

No Mutual Authentication: WEP lacks a mutual authentication mechanism, meaning that wireless clients and access points do not authenticate each other. This allows attackers to set up rogue access points without detection.

Shared Key Authentication: WEP's shared key authentication is vulnerable to attack because the challenge-response process can be exploited to reveal the key.

Weak Data Integrity: WEP's integrity check value (ICV) is only a 32-bit value, making it susceptible to tampering and data modification attacks.

5.2.2 Steps to Crack WEP Encryption

The process of cracking WEP encryption involves capturing enough data packets to reveal the encryption key. This can be accomplished using a variety of tools and techniques:

Packet Capture: Use a wireless network adapter capable of packet capture (promiscuous mode) to capture data packets from the target WEP-protected network.

Data Collection: To gather enough data for the attack, let the packet capture run for a sufficient amount of time while data traffic flows through the network.

IV Collection: During the data capture, the attacker focuses on collecting as many different IVs as possible. The limited IV space of WEP means that after enough unique IVs are captured, some IVs will start to repeat.

Cracking the Key: Once enough unique IVs are collected, the attacker can use tools like Aircrack-ng to launch a statistical attack on the WEP key. The tool analyzes the collected data packets and applies statistical techniques to determine the encryption key.

Decrypting Data: After successfully cracking the WEP key, the attacker can use it to decrypt the captured data packets, revealing the information transmitted over the network.

5.2.3 Mitigation of WEP Cracking

As WEP is highly insecure and easily crackable, it should never be used to protect wireless networks. Instead, stronger encryption protocols such as WPA2 or WPA3 should be employed. The following steps can help mitigate WEP cracking:

Upgrade Security Protocol: Replace WEP with WPA2 or WPA3, which offer stronger encryption and improved security mechanisms.

Use Strong Passwords: For WPA2 or WPA3, use strong, complex passwords or passphrases to secure the network.

Regularly Update Security Settings: Regularly update the Wi-Fi network's security settings and firmware to stay protected against known vulnerabilities.

Disable WEP: If WEP is still enabled on legacy devices or access points, disable it immediately.

Monitor Network Activity: Regularly monitor the network for any suspicious or unauthorized activity.

In conclusion, WEP encryption is no longer considered secure due to its vulnerabilities and ease of cracking. It is essential to migrate to more robust encryption standards, such as WPA2 or WPA3, to ensure the security of wireless networks. By understanding the weaknesses of WEP and taking appropriate security measures, individuals and organizations can protect their data and communications from unauthorized access and potential threats.

5.3 Attacking WPA/WPA2 Encryption

Wi-Fi Protected Access (WPA) and WPA2 are the current industry-standard encryption protocols used to secure Wi-Fi networks. Compared to the outdated WEP, they offer stronger security measures and have been designed to address the vulnerabilities present in WEP encryption. However, as with any security mechanism, WPA/WPA2 is not immune to attacks. In this section, we will explore some of the common methods used to attack WPA/WPA2 encryption and the steps to enhance the security of Wi-Fi networks.

5.3.1 WPA/WPA2 Security Features

WPA/WPA2 incorporates several security features that make it more robust than WEP:

Dynamic Encryption Keys: WPA/WPA2 uses dynamic encryption keys that change with each data packet, making it more difficult for attackers to decrypt the data.

Temporal Key Integrity Protocol (TKIP): WPA employs TKIP as the encryption protocol, which provides per-packet key mixing to counter certain types of attacks.

Advanced Encryption Standard (AES): WPA2 uses AES as the encryption protocol, which is more secure and widely adopted.

Key Management and Authentication: WPA/WPA2 incorporates 802.1X/EAP authentication, which enables strong mutual authentication between the client and the access point.

Pre-Shared Key (PSK) Mode: In PSK mode, a passphrase is used to generate the encryption key, offering convenient setup for home and small office networks.

5.3.2 Common WPA/WPA2 Attacks

Despite the stronger security of WPA/WPA2, several attacks can still compromise these networks:

Brute-Force Attack: Attackers attempt to guess the Wi-Fi network's passphrase by trying multiple combinations until the correct one is found.

Dictionary Attack: In this attack, attackers use a list of commonly used passwords and passphrases to attempt to gain access to the network.

Wi-Fi Protected Setup (WPS) Attack: WPS is a feature that allows easy setup of Wi-Fi networks. Some implementations of WPS are vulnerable to brute-force attacks.

Evil Twin Attack: Attackers set up a rogue Wi-Fi access point with a similar name to a legitimate network, tricking users into connecting to it and revealing their passphrase.

Rainbow Table Attack: Attackers use precomputed tables (rainbow tables) to quickly find the original passphrase corresponding to a captured hash.

KRACK Attack (Key Reinstallation Attack): This vulnerability in WPA/WPA2 allows attackers to reinstall an already-in-use encryption key, potentially leading to decryption of wireless traffic.

5.3.3 Securing WPA/WPA2 Networks

To enhance the security of WPA/WPA2-protected Wi-Fi networks, consider the following measures:

Use Strong Passphrases: Choose long and complex passphrases that are difficult to guess and contain a mix of upper and lower-case letters, numbers, and special characters.

Disable WPS: Disable WPS if it is not required, as it can be vulnerable to attacks.

Regularly Update Firmware: Keep the router's firmware up to date to ensure it has the latest security patches and improvements.

Enable Network Segmentation: Separate the Wi-Fi network from the main network to limit the impact of a potential breach.

Intrusion Detection/Prevention: Implement WIDS/WIPS solutions to detect and respond to suspicious activities on the Wi-Fi network.

Monitor Logins: Regularly review the logs of the Wi-Fi access points for any unauthorized login attempts.

Limit Signal Range: Adjust the Wi-Fi access point's signal strength to reduce the risk of attacks from outside the premises.

Use WPA3: For devices and access points that support it, consider upgrading to WPA3, which offers additional security enhancements.

In conclusion, while WPA/WPA2 provides more robust security than WEP, it is essential to be aware of potential vulnerabilities and the methods attackers may use to compromise these networks. By implementing strong security practices and keeping up with the latest security updates, individuals and organizations can significantly enhance the security of their Wi-Fi networks and protect sensitive data from unauthorized access.

5.4 Wireless MITM Attacks

A Man-in-the-Middle (MITM) attack is a type of cybersecurity attack where an attacker intercepts and potentially alters communication between two parties who believe they are directly communicating with each other. In the context of wireless networks, MITM attacks exploit the open nature of wireless communication to eavesdrop on, intercept, and manipulate data transmitted between wireless devices and access points. In this section, we will explore some common wireless MITM attack techniques and discuss ways to protect against them.

5.4.1 Common Wireless MITM Attack Techniques

Rogue Access Points: In a rogue access point attack, the attacker sets up a rogue wireless access point with a similar name to a legitimate network. Unsuspecting users may connect to the rogue access point, allowing the attacker to intercept their data.

Evil Twin Attack: Similar to the rogue access point attack, the evil twin attack involves creating a fake access point with the same name as a legitimate network. Users unknowingly connect to the evil twin, enabling the attacker to intercept their traffic.

ARP Spoofing/ARP Poisoning: Address Resolution Protocol (ARP) spoofing involves sending fake ARP messages to associate the attacker's MAC address with the IP address of the router or target device. This allows the attacker to intercept and manipulate data packets.

DNS Spoofing: DNS spoofing involves redirecting DNS queries to a malicious DNS server controlled by the attacker. This allows the attacker to redirect users to fake websites, leading to potential data theft.

Wi-Fi Pineapple Attack: The Wi-Fi Pineapple is a specialized device used for MITM attacks. It can perform various techniques, such as rogue access point creation and Karma attacks to intercept and manipulate wireless traffic.

KRACK Attack: The Key Reinstallation Attack (KRACK) targets the WPA/WPA2 encryption protocol. By exploiting vulnerabilities in the WPA/WPA2 handshake process, an attacker can intercept and decrypt wireless traffic.

5.4.2 Prevention and Mitigation

To protect against wireless MITM attacks, consider the following prevention and mitigation measures:

Use Strong Encryption: Deploy strong encryption protocols like WPA2 or WPA3 to secure wireless communications and protect against decryption by attackers.

Disable WPS: Disable Wi-Fi Protected Setup (WPS) if not required, as it can be vulnerable to MITM attacks.

Use Certificate-Based Authentication: Implement certificate-based authentication mechanisms for Wi-Fi networks to prevent unauthorized devices from connecting.

Public Wi-Fi Caution: Avoid connecting to unsecured or public Wi-Fi networks, as they are more susceptible to MITM attacks.

HTTPS Everywhere: Encourage the use of HTTPS for websites, as it provides end-to-end encryption, making it harder for attackers to intercept sensitive data.

Monitor for Rogue Devices: Use Wireless Intrusion Detection/Prevention Systems (WIDS/WIPS) to detect and respond to rogue access points.

Validate SSL Certificates: Always verify SSL certificates when connecting to websites to avoid falling victim to SSL stripping attacks.

ARP Spoofing Detection: Implement ARP spoofing detection mechanisms to identify and respond to ARP spoofing attacks.

Regular Software Updates: Keep devices and access points up to date with the latest security patches to protect against known vulnerabilities.

Public Key Infrastructure (PKI): Implement a PKI for managing certificates, which can enhance the security of wireless communication.

Use VPNs: Encourage the use of Virtual Private Networks (VPNs) when connecting to public Wi-Fi networks to create an encrypted tunnel for data transmission.

5.4.3 User Awareness

Educating users about the risks of wireless MITM attacks is crucial for enhancing overall security. Users should be aware of the following best practices:

Avoid Untrusted Networks: Avoid connecting to unknown or untrusted Wi-Fi networks.

Verify Network Names: Double-check the network name (SSID) to ensure it matches the legitimate network.

Use Encrypted Websites: Look for "https://" in the website URL and avoid entering sensitive information on websites without SSL encryption.

Avoid Suspicious Websites: Be cautious of websites with incorrect SSL certificates or unfamiliar URLs.

Disable Auto-Connect: Disable auto-connect to open Wi-Fi networks to prevent automatic connections to rogue access points.

In conclusion, wireless MITM attacks pose significant security risks in the open and unsecured nature of wireless communication. Implementing strong encryption, certificate-based authentication, and monitoring for rogue devices are essential steps to protect against these attacks. User awareness and caution are equally crucial to avoid falling victim to wireless MITM attacks and maintaining a secure wireless environment.

Chapter 6: Web Application Penetration Testing

Welcome to Chapter 6 of "The Kali Linux Handbook: A Practical Guide to Advanced Cybersecurity Techniques." In this chapter, we dive into the exciting realm of web application penetration testing—a critical skill for uncovering vulnerabilities in web applications and ensuring their resilience against potential cyber threats.

Web Application Security Fundamentals

Before delving into the art of web application penetration testing, we lay the foundation by understanding the key concepts of web application security. From the OWASP Top Ten vulnerabilities to common attack vectors, you'll gain insights into the prevalent risks faced by web applications and the methods used to safeguard them.

Exploiting Cross-Site Scripting (XSS) Vulnerabilities

In this section, we explore one of the most prevalent and dangerous web application vulnerabilities—Cross-Site Scripting (XSS). You'll learn how to identify and exploit XSS vulnerabilities using various techniques, including reflected and stored XSS attacks. Armed with this knowledge, you can help organizations defend against these potentially devastating security flaws.

SQL Injection Techniques

SQL Injection remains a significant threat to web applications, enabling attackers to manipulate databases and extract sensitive data. In this part, we explore SQL injection techniques using Kali Linux tools. You'll understand how to exploit these vulnerabilities and provide valuable insights to organizations on securing their database-driven applications.

Authentication and Session Management Attacks

Authentication and session management are critical aspects of web application security. In this final section, we delve into the techniques used to attack authentication mechanisms and session management functionalities. By understanding these attack vectors, you can help organizations enhance their authentication protocols and protect user sessions effectively.

Throughout this chapter, we emphasize the importance of responsible and ethical hacking. Web application penetration testing is a proactive approach to securing online services and protecting user data from potential breaches.

By mastering web application penetration testing, you'll be equipped to identify and address security flaws in web applications, bolstering the overall security posture of organizations. Let's harness the power of Kali Linux to safeguard the digital landscape and defend against web-based cyber threats.

6.1 Web Application Security Fundamentals

Web applications play a vital role in our digital lives, enabling us to perform various tasks, such as online shopping, banking, and communication. However, they are also prime targets for cyberattacks due to their widespread use and potential vulnerabilities. Web application security aims to protect these applications from threats, ensuring the confidentiality, integrity, and availability of data and services. In this section, we will explore the fundamentals of web application security and key measures to safeguard against common threats.

6.1.1 Importance of Web Application Security

Web applications are exposed to a range of security risks, including:

Injection Attacks: Malicious code (SQL injection, Cross-Site Scripting) can be injected into user inputs, leading to data theft or unauthorized access.

Cross-Site Request Forgery (CSRF): Attackers can trick users into executing unintended actions on a trusted website.

Cross-Site Script Inclusion (XSSI): Exploits weak JavaScript implementations to access sensitive data on another domain.

Session Hijacking: Attackers steal user session tokens to impersonate authenticated users.

Security Misconfigurations: Improperly configured servers or applications may expose sensitive data or functionalities.

Broken Authentication and Session Management: Weak authentication mechanisms can lead to unauthorized access.

Sensitive Data Exposure: Inadequate protection of sensitive data can result in its unauthorized disclosure.

Insecure Direct Object References (IDOR): Attackers manipulate object references to access unauthorized resources.

6.1.2 Web Application Security Best Practices

To enhance web application security, consider the following best practices:

Input Validation: Validate and sanitize all user inputs to prevent injection attacks.

Parameterized Queries: Use parameterized queries and prepared statements to avoid SQL injection vulnerabilities.

Cross-Site Scripting (XSS) Prevention: Sanitize user-generated content and use security libraries to prevent XSS attacks.

CSRF Protection: Implement anti-CSRF tokens to prevent cross-site request forgery attacks.

Secure Session Management: Use strong session management practices, including token-based authentication and secure session cookies.

HTTPS Usage: Implement HTTPS (SSL/TLS) to encrypt data transmitted between the client and the server.

Security Headers: Set appropriate security headers (e.g., Content Security Policy, X-Frame-Options) to protect against various attacks.

Access Control: Enforce proper access control mechanisms to ensure users can only access authorized resources.

Least Privilege Principle: Assign the least privilege necessary to users and limit their access to sensitive data.

Regular Security Audits: Conduct regular security audits and vulnerability assessments to identify and address potential weaknesses.

Error Handling: Implement secure error handling to prevent information leakage.

Password Management: Use strong password hashing algorithms (e.g., bcrypt) and enforce password complexity requirements.

6.1.3 Web Application Firewalls (WAFs)

A Web Application Firewall (WAF) is a security appliance or software that sits between the client and the web server, filtering and monitoring HTTP traffic. It helps protect web applications from various attacks, including SQL injection, XSS, and CSRF, by inspecting and blocking malicious requests. WAFs can be deployed as hardware appliances, virtual appliances, or cloud-based services.

6.1.4 Security Testing and Bug Bounty Programs

Security testing is essential to identify and remediate vulnerabilities in web applications. Techniques such as penetration testing, code reviews, and vulnerability scanning help assess security risks.

Bug bounty programs are initiatives that invite ethical hackers to find and report vulnerabilities in exchange for rewards. Such programs leverage the collective expertise of the security community to improve web application security.

6.1.5 Secure Software Development Lifecycle (SDLC)

A Secure Software Development Lifecycle (SDLC) incorporates security practices throughout the entire software development process. It includes security requirements, threat modeling, secure coding practices, security testing, and continuous monitoring to ensure robust application security.

In conclusion, web application security is critical to protect against the ever-evolving threat landscape. By following best practices, leveraging WAFs, conducting security testing, and integrating security throughout the SDLC, organizations can bolster their web application security posture and safeguard user data and services from malicious attacks.

6.2 Exploiting Cross-Site Scripting (XSS) Vulnerabilities

Cross-Site Scripting (XSS) is a prevalent web application security vulnerability that allows attackers to inject malicious scripts into web pages viewed by other users. When users visit the affected page, the injected scripts execute in their browsers, potentially stealing sensitive information, session hijacking, or delivering malware. XSS attacks come in various forms, each with its own specific technique and impact. In this section, we will explore how attackers exploit XSS vulnerabilities and the potential consequences of successful attacks.

6.2.1 Types of XSS Attacks

XSS attacks can be categorized into three main types:

Stored XSS: Also known as persistent or permanent XSS, this type occurs when the malicious script is permanently stored on the target server. The script is served to every user who accesses the vulnerable page, making it more dangerous and widespread.

Reflected XSS: In a reflected XSS attack, the injected script is reflected off a web server or another user's input and executed directly in the victim's browser. This type is commonly seen in URLs or search queries.

DOM-based XSS: This type of XSS occurs when the client-side scripts manipulate the Document Object Model (DOM) of a web page. The malicious script modifies the page's structure or content, leading to code execution in the victim's browser.

6.2.2 Steps to Exploit XSS Vulnerabilities

To exploit an XSS vulnerability, attackers follow these general steps:

Identify Vulnerable Input Points: First, the attacker identifies input fields, such as search boxes, login forms, or comment sections, where user-supplied data is not adequately sanitized before being displayed on the page.

Inject Malicious Script: The attacker then crafts a malicious script, typically JavaScript, and injects it into the vulnerable input field.

Persistence (Stored XSS): If the vulnerability allows for stored XSS, the attacker submits the input containing the malicious script to the server. The script is now stored on the server and served to every user who views the page.

Triggering the Attack: In the case of reflected or DOM-based XSS, the attacker shares the malicious URL or crafted input with potential victims. When users access the manipulated URL or input, the script executes in their browsers.

Exploiting the User: The malicious script can perform various actions, such as stealing session cookies, redirecting to phishing sites, or performing actions on behalf of the user without their consent.

6.2.3 Consequences of Successful XSS Attacks

The consequences of a successful XSS attack can be severe:

Session Hijacking: Attackers can steal session cookies or tokens, allowing them to impersonate the victim and gain unauthorized access to their accounts.

Data Theft: XSS attacks can be used to exfiltrate sensitive information, such as login credentials, personal data, or financial details.

Phishing Attacks: Attackers can redirect users to malicious websites designed to trick them into divulging sensitive information.

Defacement: In stored XSS attacks, attackers can modify the content of web pages, leading to website defacement and loss of credibility.

Delivering Malware: Malicious scripts can deliver malware or initiate drive-by downloads, infecting users' devices.

Brute-Force Attacks: Attackers can use XSS to perform automated brute-force attacks on login forms.

6.2.4 Preventing XSS Attacks

To prevent XSS attacks, web developers and organizations should follow best practices:

Input Validation and Sanitization: Validate and sanitize all user inputs to prevent malicious code from being executed.

Use Context-Aware Escaping: Use context-aware escaping based on the location where data is rendered to avoid incorrect sanitization.

Content Security Policy (CSP): Implement CSP headers to restrict the sources of executable scripts and mitigate XSS risks.

HTTP Only and Secure Flags: Set the HTTP Only and Secure flags on session cookies to prevent client-side scripts from accessing sensitive data.

Use Security Libraries: Utilize security libraries and frameworks that automatically handle input sanitization.

Regular Security Audits: Conduct regular security audits and penetration tests to identify and fix potential XSS vulnerabilities.

Stay Updated: Keep web applications and frameworks up to date with the latest security patches and updates.

By implementing these preventive measures, organizations can significantly reduce the risk of XSS attacks and enhance the security of their web applications.

6.3 SQL Injection Techniques

SQL Injection is a type of cybersecurity attack where an attacker maliciously inserts or manipulates SQL queries in a web application's input fields to gain unauthorized access to the underlying database. This security vulnerability arises when the application fails to properly validate or sanitize user inputs before using them in SQL queries. Successful SQL injection attacks can have severe consequences, such as unauthorized data access, data manipulation, and potentially full control of the application's database. In this section, we will explore common SQL injection techniques used by attackers and ways to prevent such attacks.

6.3.1 SQL Injection Attack Types

SQL injection attacks can be broadly categorized into three main types:

Classic SQL Injection: In classic SQL injection, the attacker injects malicious SQL code into the application's input fields, such as login forms or search boxes, which then gets executed by the application's backend database.

Blind SQL Injection: In blind SQL injection, the attacker does not directly see the results of the injected query. However, by using boolean-based or time-based techniques, they can infer the information from the application's response.

Second-Order SQL Injection: In this type of attack, the injected SQL code does not execute immediately. Instead, it gets stored in the application's database, and later, when accessed by another part of the application, it executes, potentially causing damage.

6.3.2 SQL Injection Techniques

Attackers use various techniques to perform SQL injection attacks:

Union-Based SQL Injection: The attacker appends a UNION statement to the input, tricking the application into combining their malicious query with the original one, and returns combined results.

Boolean-Based SQL Injection: The attacker exploits boolean conditions in SQL queries to infer information about the database. By manipulating the application's response, they can determine whether certain conditions are true or false.

Time-Based Blind SQL Injection: In time-based blind SQL injection, the attacker injects malicious queries that cause a delay in the application's response. By observing the delay, they can infer if the injected condition is true or false.

Error-Based SQL Injection: The attacker injects code that intentionally produces errors in the SQL query. The application's error messages then reveal valuable information about the database structure.

Out-of-Band (OOB) SQL Injection: In OOB SQL injection, the attacker sends data to a remote server controlled by them through DNS requests or HTTP requests. This allows them to extract data even if the application does not return query results directly.

Stored Procedure Injection: Attackers can manipulate stored procedures in the application's database to execute malicious code.

6.3.3 Preventing SQL Injection Attacks

Preventing SQL injection attacks requires adopting secure coding practices and implementing preventive measures:

Parameterized Queries (Prepared Statements): Use parameterized queries or prepared statements with placeholders to pass user inputs safely to the database.

Stored Procedures: Use stored procedures to control database access and avoid dynamic SQL queries.

Input Validation and Sanitization: Validate and sanitize all user inputs to prevent malicious data from entering the application.

Least Privilege Principle: Ensure that database accounts used by the application have the least privilege necessary to perform their tasks.

Web Application Firewall (WAF): Implement a WAF to detect and block SQL injection attempts.

Security Audits and Code Reviews: Regularly conduct security audits and code reviews to identify and fix potential SQL injection vulnerabilities.

Error Handling: Implement secure error handling to avoid exposing sensitive information in error messages.

Database Firewall: Consider using a database firewall to monitor and block suspicious database activity.

User Input Restrictions: Implement strict restrictions on user input, allowing only the necessary characters and length.

By adopting these preventive measures, organizations can significantly reduce the risk of SQL injection attacks and ensure the security and integrity of their web applications and databases.

6.4 Authentication and Session Management Attacks

Authentication and session management are critical components of web application security. Properly implemented, they ensure that users are who they claim to be and maintain secure user sessions during their interactions with the application. However, if not adequately protected, these areas can be exploited by attackers to gain unauthorized access to user accounts, compromise sensitive data, or perform malicious activities. In this section, we will explore common authentication and session management attacks and best practices to mitigate their risks.

6.4.1 Common Authentication Attacks

Brute-Force Attack: Attackers attempt to gain access to user accounts by systematically trying various password combinations until they find the correct one.

Credential Stuffing: Attackers use username-password pairs obtained from previous data breaches to gain unauthorized access to other applications, assuming users reuse passwords.

Password Guessing: Attackers try to guess weak passwords based on common patterns or publicly available information about the user.

Phishing: In phishing attacks, attackers create deceptive websites or emails to trick users into disclosing their login credentials.

Man-in-the-Middle (MITM) Attack: Attackers intercept communication between the user and the server to steal authentication credentials.

Session Fixation: Attackers force users to use a predetermined session ID, allowing them to hijack the user's session after login.

6.4.2 Best Practices for Authentication Security

To prevent authentication attacks, consider the following best practices:

Strong Password Policies: Enforce strong password policies, requiring passwords to have a mix of uppercase and lowercase letters, numbers, and special characters.

Multi-Factor Authentication (MFA): Implement MFA to add an extra layer of security, requiring users to provide additional verification, such as a one-time code sent to their mobile device.

Account Lockout Policy: Implement an account lockout policy to prevent brute-force attacks by locking out accounts after a certain number of failed login attempts.

CAPTCHA: Use CAPTCHA or reCAPTCHA to distinguish between human users and automated bots during authentication.

Secure Login Forms: Ensure login forms are secure and use HTTPS to encrypt login credentials during transmission.

User Awareness: Educate users about the importance of strong passwords, the risks of phishing, and safe online practices.

6.4.3 Common Session Management Attacks

Session Hijacking: Attackers steal or guess session identifiers to impersonate authenticated users and gain unauthorized access to their accounts.

Session Fixation: In session fixation attacks, attackers set a user's session ID to a known value, making it possible for them to take over the session after the user logs in.

Session Replay: Attackers capture and replay a user's session data to gain unauthorized access to the application.

Session Expiration and Timeout: Attackers exploit sessions that do not have proper expiration and idle timeout mechanisms, allowing them to access active sessions after the user leaves the application.

6.4.4 Best Practices for Session Management Security

To enhance session management security, consider the following best practices:

Secure Session IDs: Use cryptographically strong and unpredictable session IDs to reduce the risk of session guessing and fixation attacks.

Session Expiration: Set appropriate session expiration times to limit the duration of active sessions.

Idle Timeout: Implement an idle timeout mechanism to automatically log out users after a period of inactivity.

Session Revocation: Enable the ability to invalidate or revoke sessions when a user logs out or when suspicious activity is detected.

HTTPS: Always use HTTPS to secure the transmission of session data between the client and server.

Secure Cookies: Use HTTP-only and secure flags for cookies to prevent client-side scripts from accessing sensitive session data.

Audit and Monitoring: Regularly audit and monitor session activity to detect and respond to suspicious behavior.

In conclusion, robust authentication and session management practices are essential for ensuring the security of web applications. By implementing strong authentication mechanisms, employing MFA, and following best practices for session management, organizations can mitigate the risks of authentication and session-related attacks and safeguard their users' data and accounts.

Chapter 7: Network Sniffing and Spoofing

Welcome to Chapter 7 of "The Kali Linux Handbook: A Practical Guide to Advanced Cybersecurity Techniques." In this chapter, we dive into the intriguing world of network sniffing and spoofing—an essential skill for understanding network traffic and uncovering potential security risks.

Capturing Network Traffic with Wireshark

We begin by exploring the powerful tool, Wireshark, a renowned network protocol analyzer. You'll learn how to capture and analyze network traffic to gain insights into the data exchanged between devices. By understanding network protocols and dissecting packets, you'll be able to identify anomalies and potential security breaches.

Analyzing Captured Packets

In this section, we take a closer look at the data captured by Wireshark and learn how to interpret and analyze packet contents effectively. By examining the information within packets, you'll develop a deeper understanding of network behaviors and potential security weaknesses.

Spoofing MAC Addresses with Macchanger

MAC address spoofing is a technique used to change the hardware address of a network interface. In this part, we explore the tool, Macchanger, which enables us to change MAC addresses to remain undetected or bypass network access controls. You'll learn the implications of MAC address spoofing and how to protect against such attacks.

ARP Spoofing and DNS Spoofing

ARP Spoofing and DNS Spoofing are potent techniques used in man-in-the-middle attacks. In this final section, we delve into these methods and understand how attackers manipulate the Address Resolution Protocol (ARP) and Domain Name System (DNS) to intercept and manipulate network communications. By mastering these techniques, you can help organizations defend against MITM attacks and secure their network traffic.

Throughout this chapter, we emphasize the ethical use of network sniffing and spoofing techniques. The goal is to understand network behaviors, detect potential security threats, and improve network security—never to engage in malicious activities.

By mastering network sniffing and spoofing, you'll be better equipped to safeguard networks, ensuring secure and reliable data transmission. Let's harness the power of Kali Linux to bolster network defenses and protect against potential cyber intrusions.

7.1 Capturing Network Traffic with Wireshark

Wireshark is a popular open-source network protocol analyzer that allows users to capture and inspect network traffic. It is a powerful tool used by network administrators, security professionals, and researchers to analyze and troubleshoot network issues, as well as to identify security threats and vulnerabilities. In this section, we will explore the process of capturing network traffic using Wireshark and some essential features of the tool.

7.1.1 Installing Wireshark

Before capturing network traffic with Wireshark, you need to install the software on your computer. Wireshark is available for various operating systems, including Windows, macOS, and Linux. You can download the latest version of Wireshark from the official website (www.wireshark.org) and follow the installation instructions specific to your operating system.

7.1.2 Capturing Network Traffic

Once Wireshark is installed, you can start capturing network traffic by following these steps:

Open Wireshark: Launch the Wireshark application on your computer.

Select the Network Interface: In the main Wireshark window, you will see a list of available network interfaces. Select the interface through which you want to capture the network traffic. For example, if you want to capture traffic from your Ethernet connection, select the Ethernet interface. If you want to capture Wi-Fi traffic, choose the appropriate Wi-Fi interface.

Start Capturing: Click on the "Start" button (a green shark fin icon) to begin capturing network traffic. Wireshark will start capturing packets in real-time.

Analyze the Traffic: As Wireshark captures packets, you will see them displayed in the main window. You can analyze the packets by inspecting the different fields, such as source and destination IP addresses, protocols, payload data, and more.

Stop Capturing: To stop the packet capture, click on the "Stop" button (a red square icon) in Wireshark.

7.1.3 Capturing Specific Traffic

Wireshark allows you to filter the captured traffic to focus on specific packets of interest. You can apply display filters to show only certain types of packets based on criteria such as source or destination IP address, port numbers, protocols, and more. To apply a display filter, use the filter bar at the top of the Wireshark window and enter the filter expression. For example, to display only HTTP traffic, you can enter "http" in the filter bar.

7.1.4 Saving Captured Traffic

Wireshark gives you the option to save the captured packets for later analysis. To save the captured traffic, go to "File" in the menu and select "Save" or "Save As." You can save the capture in the standard PCAP format, which can be opened and analyzed later in Wireshark or other network analysis tools.

7.1.5 Analyzing Captured Traffic

Once you have captured and saved the network traffic, you can analyze it further using various features of Wireshark. You can use features like color coding, packet coloring rules, and statistics to identify patterns and anomalies in the captured data. Additionally, Wireshark provides various analysis tools for specific protocols and network behaviors.

7.1.6 Important Considerations

Capturing network traffic with Wireshark requires appropriate permissions on your system, and in some cases, you may need administrative privileges. Additionally, capturing network traffic on a network you do not own or without proper authorization may violate privacy and security laws, so always ensure you have permission to capture network traffic on the specific network.

In conclusion, Wireshark is a valuable tool for capturing and analyzing network traffic. Whether you are troubleshooting network issues or investigating security incidents, Wireshark provides deep insights into the communication occurring on your network, helping you understand network behavior and detect potential threats.

7.2 Analyzing Captured Packets

After capturing network packets with Wireshark, the real power of the tool comes into play during the analysis phase. Wireshark provides a rich set of features to dissect and interpret captured packets, enabling network administrators, security professionals, and researchers to gain valuable insights into network behavior, troubleshoot issues, and detect security threats. In this section, we will explore how to analyze captured packets using Wireshark.

7.2.1 Displaying Captured Packets

Once you have captured network packets and saved them in a PCAP file, you can open the file in Wireshark to start the analysis. To do this, launch Wireshark and go to "File" in the menu, then select "Open." Browse to the location of the saved PCAP file and click "Open." Wireshark will load the captured packets, and you will see them displayed in the main window.

7.2.2 Packet List Pane

The Packet List pane is the central area of the Wireshark window, showing a list of all captured packets. Each row in the list represents a single packet, and the columns display various details, such as the packet number, time of capture, source and destination addresses, protocol used, and packet length.

7.2.3 Packet Detail Pane

The Packet Detail pane in Wireshark displays the dissected contents of the selected packet from the Packet List pane. Here, you can see the various protocol layers of the packet, including Ethernet, IP, TCP/UDP, and application layer protocols. By expanding each layer, you can inspect the specific fields and data within the packet.

7.2.4 Filtering Packets

Wireshark allows you to apply various filters to focus on specific packets of interest. Filters can be based on various criteria, such as IP addresses, protocols, port numbers, and specific packet contents. To apply a filter, use the filter bar at the top of the Wireshark window and enter the filter expression. For example, to display only HTTP traffic, you can enter "http" in the filter bar.

7.2.5 Coloring Rules

Wireshark uses color coding to highlight packets based on specific criteria. For example, successful TCP connections may be colored green, while packets with errors or anomalies could be colored red. You can customize the coloring rules in Wireshark to suit your analysis requirements.

7.2.6 Packet Statistics

Wireshark provides various statistics and analysis tools to gain insights into network behavior. To access packet statistics, go to "Statistics" in the menu and select the desired analysis category, such as Protocol Hierarchy, Conversations, or Endpoints. These statistics help identify traffic patterns, detect unusual behavior, and analyze the distribution of protocols and data across the network.

7.2.7 Expert Information

Wireshark includes an "Expert Info" feature that provides alerts and warnings about potential issues in captured packets. The Expert Info pane displays warnings related to packet errors, retransmissions, out-of-order packets, and other anomalies. These alerts help pinpoint network problems and possible security threats.

7.2.8 Follow TCP Stream

The "Follow TCP Stream" feature in Wireshark allows you to view the entire content of a TCP conversation. Right-click on a TCP packet in the Packet List pane, then select "Follow" and "TCP Stream." This will display the complete TCP data stream for that conversation, making it easier to understand the communication between client and server.

7.2.9 Exporting Data

Wireshark allows you to export packets or selected packet details to various formats, such as CSV, XML, or plain text. This can be useful for further analysis in other tools or for generating reports.

In conclusion, analyzing captured packets with Wireshark is a fundamental skill for understanding network behavior and diagnosing network issues. By leveraging the many features and tools available in

Wireshark, network professionals can gain valuable insights into their network traffic, enhance security monitoring, and ensure the smooth operation of their networks.

7.3 Spoofing MAC Addresses with Macchanger

Macchanger is a command-line tool available on Linux systems that allows users to change or spoof the Media Access Control (MAC) address of their network interface cards (NICs). MAC address spoofing can be used for various purposes, such as enhancing privacy, bypassing network restrictions, or conducting ethical hacking and security testing. In this section, we will explore how to use Macchanger to spoof MAC addresses on a Linux system.

7.3.1 Installing Macchanger

Macchanger is typically available in the package repositories of most Linux distributions. To install Macchanger, open a terminal and use the package manager specific to your distribution. For example, on Debian/Ubuntu-based systems, use:

sudo apt-get install macchanger

On Fedora/RHEL-based systems, use:

sudo dnf install macchanger

7.3.2 Checking Current MAC Address

Before spoofing the MAC address, it's a good idea to check the current MAC address of your network interface. In the terminal, use the following command to view the MAC address of a specific interface (replace "interface_name" with the actual interface name, e.g., wlan0 or eth0):

ifconfig interface_name | grep "ether"

Alternatively, you can use the "ip" command:

ip link show interface_name

7.3.3 Spoofing the MAC Address

Once you have Macchanger installed, you can use it to spoof the MAC address of your network interface. To do this, follow these steps:

Disable the Interface: Before changing the MAC address, ensure that the network interface is down. You can use the following command to bring down the interface (replace "interface_name" with the actual interface name):

sudo ifconfig interface_name down

Spoof the MAC Address: Use Macchanger to spoof the MAC address of the interface with the following command (replace "interface_name" with the actual interface name):

sudo macchanger -r interface_name

The "-r" option tells Macchanger to generate a random MAC address and assign it to the interface.

Bring Up the Interface: After spoofing the MAC address, bring the interface back up with the following command:

sudo ifconfig interface_name up

7.3.4 Verifying the Spoofed MAC Address

To verify that the MAC address has been successfully spoofed, use the same commands mentioned earlier to check the current MAC address of the interface.

7.3.5 Reverting to the Original MAC Address

If you want to revert to the original MAC address of the interface, simply bring down the interface, and then use Macchanger to set the original MAC address:

sudo ifconfig interface_name down

sudo macchanger -p interface_name
sudo ifconfig interface_name up

The "-p" option tells Macchanger to set the permanent MAC address (original MAC address) of the interface.

7.3.6 Important Considerations

Spoofing MAC addresses may violate the terms of service of certain networks or be illegal in some jurisdictions. Always ensure you have the proper authorization to change MAC addresses on a network.

Additionally, keep in mind that MAC address spoofing is not a foolproof method of anonymity or security. Other methods of tracking and identification may still be used by network administrators or attackers.

In conclusion, Macchanger provides a simple and convenient way to spoof MAC addresses on Linux systems. However, it should be used responsibly and ethically, with full awareness of the potential consequences and legal implications.

7.4 ARP Spoofing and DNS Spoofing

ARP (Address Resolution Protocol) spoofing and DNS (Domain Name System) spoofing are two types of cyberattacks that manipulate network protocols to redirect traffic or impersonate network devices. These attacks are commonly used for malicious purposes, such as eavesdropping, man-in-the-middle attacks, and stealing sensitive information. Understanding these attack techniques is crucial for network administrators and security professionals to protect their networks effectively. In this section, we will explore ARP spoofing and DNS spoofing, their methods, and potential mitigation strategies.

7.4.1 ARP Spoofing

ARP is a protocol used to map IP addresses to MAC addresses on a local network. ARP spoofing, also known as ARP poisoning or ARP cache poisoning, is an attack where an attacker sends falsified ARP messages to associate their MAC address with the IP address of another legitimate device on the network.

Method of ARP Spoofing:

The attacker starts by sending forged ARP messages to the local network, claiming that their MAC address is associated with the IP address of the network gateway (e.g., the router).

Other devices on the network, believing the forged ARP messages, update their ARP caches with the attacker's MAC address as the gateway's MAC address.

As a result, all traffic that should be sent to the gateway is redirected to the attacker's machine.

The attacker can intercept, inspect, or modify the traffic before forwarding it to the actual gateway, making it a man-in-the-middle attack.

Mitigation of ARP Spoofing:

ARP Spoofing Detection Tools: Use network monitoring tools that can detect and alert on ARP spoofing activities, helping to identify potential attackers.

Static ARP Entries: Manually configure static ARP entries on critical network devices to prevent ARP cache poisoning.

ARP Spoofing Prevention Tools: Deploy security tools or configure network devices that actively prevent ARP spoofing attacks.

Network Segmentation: Implement network segmentation to reduce the impact of ARP spoofing attacks by isolating critical network segments.

7.4.2 DNS Spoofing

DNS is responsible for resolving human-readable domain names into IP addresses. DNS spoofing, also known as DNS cache poisoning or DNS poisoning, is an attack where an attacker manipulates DNS responses to redirect users to malicious websites or unauthorized IP addresses.

Method of DNS Spoofing:

The attacker exploits a vulnerability in the DNS server or its configuration to inject falsified DNS responses into the server's cache.

When a legitimate user makes a DNS query for a specific domain name, the DNS server responds with the falsified IP address, directing the user to a malicious website.

The user's system stores the falsified DNS response in its local DNS cache, leading to subsequent requests being redirected to the attacker-controlled IP address.

As a result, the attacker can intercept, modify, or monitor the user's traffic, potentially leading to further attacks.

Mitigation of DNS Spoofing:

DNSSEC (DNS Security Extensions): DNSSEC is a suite of extensions to DNS that adds an additional layer of security by digitally signing DNS data. Implement DNSSEC to ensure DNS data integrity and authenticity.

Source Port Randomization: Configure the DNS server to use source port randomization, which makes it harder for attackers to guess the DNS transaction ID and forge responses.

DNS Caching Best Practices: Configure DNS servers to minimize caching of external DNS responses, reducing the window of opportunity for DNS spoofing.

Firewalls and Intrusion Detection Systems (IDS): Use firewalls and IDS to monitor and block suspicious DNS traffic and potential DNS spoofing attempts.

In conclusion, ARP spoofing and DNS spoofing are dangerous attack techniques that can lead to significant security breaches and privacy violations. By understanding these attack methods and implementing appropriate mitigation strategies, network administrators and security professionals can enhance the security of their networks and protect against these types of attacks.

Chapter 8: Post-Exploitation Techniques

Welcome to Chapter 8 of "The Kali Linux Handbook: A Practical Guide to Advanced Cybersecurity Techniques." In this pivotal chapter, we delve into the critical phase of post-exploitation—an essential skill for maintaining access, escalating privileges, and covering tracks after a successful cyber intrusion.

Escalating Privileges with Linux

In this section, we explore the art of privilege escalation in Linux systems. You'll learn how to identify and exploit vulnerabilities that allow you to elevate your privileges from a standard user to a privileged user, such as root. Understanding these techniques is crucial for gaining full control over a compromised system.

Escalating Privileges with Windows

Windows systems present unique challenges for privilege escalation. In this part, we explore the techniques used to escalate privileges on Windows machines. From exploiting misconfigurations to bypassing access controls, you'll gain insights into how attackers navigate the Windows environment to gain administrative rights.

Maintaining Persistent Access

Once you've successfully compromised a system, maintaining persistent access is essential to ensure ongoing control. In this section, we delve into various methods for establishing backdoors and maintaining access even after system reboots or security measures have been applied.

Covering Tracks and Erasing Evidence

In this final section, we explore the art of covering tracks and erasing evidence to avoid detection. From removing logs and erasing command histories to concealing the presence of malicious activity, you'll learn how to clean up after a successful cyber intrusion.

Throughout this chapter, we stress the importance of using post-exploitation techniques responsibly and ethically. Understanding these methods empowers cybersecurity professionals to defend against them effectively and helps organizations implement countermeasures to detect and respond to potential cyber threats.

By mastering post-exploitation techniques, you'll gain a deeper understanding of cyber attackers' motives and strategies, enabling you to bolster your organization's defenses and protect against persistent threats.

Let's embrace the responsibilities of ethical hacking and explore the world of post-exploitation techniques, fortifying our cybersecurity expertise and safeguarding the digital landscape.

8.1 Escalating Privileges with Linux

Privilege escalation is the process of gaining higher-level access or permissions on a system than what is originally granted to a user. In Linux systems, there are various techniques and vulnerabilities that attackers may exploit to escalate privileges from a standard user to a privileged user (like root). Understanding these techniques is essential for both system administrators to secure their systems and security professionals to defend against potential attacks. In this section, we will explore some common privilege escalation methods in Linux and methods to mitigate them.

8.1.1 Exploiting Vulnerabilities

Kernel Exploits: Attackers may search for vulnerabilities in the Linux kernel to gain kernel-level privileges. These vulnerabilities can allow them to execute arbitrary code with elevated privileges.

Software Vulnerabilities: Exploiting vulnerabilities in setuid-root programs or other software running with elevated privileges is another common method for privilege escalation.

Mitigation: Keep the system up-to-date with the latest security patches and updates. Regularly monitor security advisories and promptly apply patches to fix known vulnerabilities.

8.1.2 Misconfigured File Permissions

Sensitive Configuration Files: If sensitive configuration files have incorrect permissions, attackers can modify them to gain elevated privileges.

Writable Directories: If directories where executables are stored have world-writable permissions, attackers can replace binaries with malicious ones to gain privilege escalation.

Mitigation: Follow the principle of least privilege. Set appropriate permissions for sensitive files and directories, ensuring they are only accessible by authorized users.

8.1.3 Weak Service Configurations

Insecure Services: Misconfigured services or daemons that run with root privileges can be exploited to gain elevated access.

Weak Service Accounts: Weak or default credentials for service accounts may provide an entry point for attackers.

Mitigation: Disable unnecessary services and configure remaining services securely. Use strong, unique passwords for service accounts and avoid using default credentials.

8.1.4 Sudo Misconfigurations

Unrestricted Sudo Access: If a user is granted unrestricted sudo access to run specific commands, attackers may abuse this to run arbitrary commands with root privileges.

Sudo Vulnerabilities: Exploiting vulnerabilities in the sudo configuration can also lead to privilege escalation.

Mitigation: Limit sudo access to only essential commands required by users. Use "sudo -l" to review the sudo permissions of users on the system.

8.1.5 Insecure Environment Variables

LD_PRELOAD: The LD_PRELOAD environment variable can be manipulated to load malicious libraries and escalate privileges.

PATH Manipulation: Modifying the PATH environment variable can lead to the execution of a malicious binary before the legitimate one, resulting in privilege escalation.

Mitigation: Avoid setting insecure environment variables. Use absolute paths when calling binaries to prevent PATH-related attacks.

8.1.6 Kernel Modules and Drivers

Loadable Kernel Modules: Attackers may exploit vulnerable or malicious loadable kernel modules to escalate privileges.

Malicious Device Drivers: Insecure or malicious device drivers can also be exploited for privilege escalation.

Mitigation: Limit the loading of kernel modules to trusted sources. Regularly audit kernel modules and monitor for any unauthorized changes.

In conclusion, privilege escalation is a serious security concern in Linux systems. Understanding the various methods used by attackers to escalate privileges and implementing appropriate security measures are essential to protect sensitive data and maintain the integrity of the system. Regularly auditing and patching the system, configuring permissions securely, and following the principle of least privilege can significantly reduce the risk of privilege escalation attacks.

8.2 Escalating Privileges with Windows

Privilege escalation is a critical security concern on Windows systems, as it allows attackers to gain higher-level access or permissions than what is originally granted to a user. Windows operating systems have various vulnerabilities and misconfigurations that attackers may exploit to escalate privileges from a standard user to an administrator or system-level user. Understanding these techniques is crucial for both system administrators to secure their systems and security professionals to defend against potential attacks. In this section, we will explore some common privilege escalation methods on Windows and methods to mitigate them.

8.2.1 Exploiting Vulnerabilities

Zero-Day Exploits: Attackers may use unknown vulnerabilities in Windows components or third-party software to escalate privileges.

Weak Permissions: Insecure file or registry permissions can allow attackers to modify critical system files or settings, leading to privilege escalation.

Mitigation: Keep Windows and third-party software up-to-date with the latest security patches and updates. Regularly monitor security advisories and promptly apply patches to fix known vulnerabilities.

8.2.2 Misconfigured User Account Control (UAC)

Bypassing UAC Prompts: Attackers may use social engineering or techniques like DLL hijacking to bypass UAC prompts and execute code with elevated privileges.

UAC Whitelisting Bypass: Some applications may be whitelisted in UAC settings, allowing them to run with elevated privileges without a prompt.

Mitigation: Configure UAC settings appropriately and avoid adding unnecessary applications to UAC whitelists. Educate users about UAC prompts and the importance of not blindly allowing elevation.

8.2.3 Weak Service Configurations

Insecure Services: Misconfigured services or daemons running with high privileges can be exploited to gain elevated access.

Weak Service Accounts: Weak or default credentials for service accounts may provide an entry point for attackers.

Mitigation: Disable unnecessary services and configure remaining services securely. Use strong, unique passwords for service accounts and avoid using default credentials.

8.2.4 Exploiting Scheduled Tasks

Insecure Scheduled Tasks: Misconfigured scheduled tasks can allow attackers to run arbitrary code with elevated privileges.

Overprivileged Tasks: Some scheduled tasks may run with higher privileges than necessary, creating an opportunity for privilege escalation.

Mitigation: Review and validate scheduled tasks regularly. Limit the privileges of tasks to the minimum required for their functionality.

8.2.5 Registry Hijacking

DLL Sideloading: Attackers may use vulnerable applications that load DLLs from insecure locations, allowing them to hijack the loading of a malicious DLL and escalate privileges.

Registry Key Permissions: Incorrect permissions on registry keys can lead to privilege escalation if attackers modify critical settings.

Mitigation: Use secure practices when deploying and configuring applications that involve DLL loading. Set appropriate permissions on sensitive registry keys.

8.2.6 Kerberos Ticket Attacks

Pass-the-Ticket (PtT) Attack: Attackers can use PtT attacks to steal Kerberos tickets and gain unauthorized access with the victim's credentials.

Overpass-the-Hash (PtH) Attack: PtH attacks involve using hashed credentials to impersonate a user and escalate privileges.

Mitigation: Monitor for suspicious Kerberos activity and enforce strong password policies. Implement solutions that detect and prevent PtT and PtH attacks.

In conclusion, privilege escalation is a significant threat on Windows systems. Implementing strong security practices, regularly auditing system configurations, and staying vigilant about security updates can help mitigate the risk of privilege escalation attacks. Additionally, user education and awareness are essential to prevent social engineering techniques that may lead to privilege escalation.

8.3 Maintaining Persistent Access

After gaining unauthorized access to a system through privilege escalation or other means, attackers often seek to maintain their foothold to ensure long-term access and control over the compromised system. This process is known as maintaining persistent access. By establishing persistence, attackers can return to the compromised system even if the initial point of entry is discovered and patched. Understanding common techniques used to maintain persistent access is crucial for cybersecurity professionals to detect and prevent ongoing attacks. In this section, we will explore some common methods employed by attackers to maintain persistent access and strategies to mitigate these threats.

8.3.1 Backdoors and Malware

Backdoors: Attackers may install backdoors—hidden access points or functionality—on the compromised system, providing them with an entry point for future access even if the original vulnerability is patched.

Rootkits: Rootkits are malicious software that grant privileged access and hide their presence from the operating system and security tools, making detection challenging.

Mitigation: Regularly scan systems for signs of suspicious files or unexpected network connections.

Implement strong endpoint protection solutions that can detect and remove malware and rootkits.

8.3.2 Scheduled Tasks and Cron Jobs

Scheduled Tasks: Attackers may create malicious scheduled tasks on Windows or cron jobs on Linux to execute code at predefined intervals, ensuring their continued presence.

Mitigation: Regularly review and validate scheduled tasks or cron jobs. Limit the privileges of scheduled tasks to the minimum required for their functionality.

8.3.3 Registry Modifications

Registry Persistence: Attackers may modify specific registry keys to execute malicious code during system startup or user logon, maintaining persistence.

Mitigation: Monitor critical registry keys for unauthorized changes and enforce strict access controls on sensitive registry entries.

8.3.4 Malicious Services

Unauthorized Services: Attackers may create new services on the compromised system to automatically execute their malicious code upon system startup.

Mitigation: Regularly review the list of installed services and ensure that only authorized and necessary services are running.

8.3.5 Credential Theft

Credential Dumping: Attackers may use tools to dump credentials from the compromised system, allowing them to obtain passwords and access credentials of users and administrators.

Mitigation: Implement strong password policies, use multi-factor authentication, and regularly monitor for signs of credential dumping.

8.3.6 Steganography

Hidden Data: Attackers may use steganography techniques to hide malicious code or data within seemingly innocent files, such as images or documents.

Mitigation: Employ security solutions that can detect and analyze suspicious files for hidden or obfuscated content.

8.3.7 Tunneling and Pivot Points

Tunneling: Attackers may create encrypted tunnels to exfiltrate data or control the compromised system from a remote location.

Pivot Points: Attackers may use compromised systems as pivot points to move laterally within the network and gain access to other systems.

Mitigation: Monitor network traffic for signs of tunneling and lateral movement. Implement network segmentation to limit the impact of compromised systems.

8.3.8 System Firmware and BIOS

Firmware and BIOS Attacks: Attackers may target system firmware and BIOS to implant malicious code that survives operating system reinstallation.

Mitigation: Keep system firmware and BIOS up-to-date with the latest security patches. Enable BIOS protection mechanisms, if available.

In conclusion, maintaining persistent access is a critical goal for attackers seeking to maintain control over compromised systems. Cybersecurity professionals must remain vigilant, regularly monitor systems for signs of compromise, and implement security measures to detect and prevent persistent access. Regular audits, strong access controls, and endpoint security solutions are essential components of a comprehensive defense strategy against persistent threats.

8.4 Covering Tracks and Erasing Evidence

After successfully compromising a system, attackers often try to cover their tracks and erase evidence of their activities to avoid detection and forensic investigation. By removing traces of their presence, attackers can delay or prevent security teams from identifying the breach and understanding the extent of the damage. Understanding common techniques used by attackers to cover tracks and erase evidence is essential for cybersecurity professionals to detect ongoing attacks and conduct effective incident response. In this section, we will explore some common methods employed by attackers to cover tracks and erase evidence, as well as strategies to mitigate these threats.

8.4.1 Log Manipulation and Deletion

Clearing Logs: Attackers may delete or clear system logs, security event logs, and audit logs to remove any records of their activities.

Log Tampering: In some cases, attackers may modify log entries to hide their actions or inject false information.

Mitigation: Implement centralized logging and securely store log files on a separate server with restricted access. Regularly monitor log files for unusual activity and ensure that log integrity is maintained.

8.4.2 File Deletion and Shredding

Deleting Incriminating Files: Attackers may delete files and tools used during the attack to remove evidence of their activities.

File Shredding: Instead of traditional deletion, attackers may use file-shredding techniques to overwrite data multiple times to make recovery more difficult.

Mitigation: Enable file system auditing to monitor file deletion activities. Implement data backup solutions to ensure that critical data can be recovered if necessary.

8.4.3 Anti-Forensics Tools

Covering Tracks Tools: Attackers may use specialized tools designed to clean up logs, delete traces, and conceal their presence.

Anti-Forensics Techniques: Some attackers may employ anti-forensics techniques to disrupt or hinder forensic investigations.

Mitigation: Deploy endpoint security solutions that can detect and prevent the use of anti-forensics tools. Conduct regular security audits to identify potential vulnerabilities.

8.4.4 Encryption and Data Exfiltration

Data Encryption: Attackers may use encryption to obfuscate stolen data or communications, making it more challenging to identify sensitive information.

Data Exfiltration: To avoid detection, attackers may use encrypted channels to exfiltrate stolen data from the compromised system.

Mitigation: Monitor network traffic for suspicious encrypted communications. Implement data loss prevention (DLP) solutions to detect and prevent data exfiltration.

8.4.5 Time Stomping

Time Stomping: Attackers may alter file timestamps (creation, modification, and access times) to mislead investigators about the timing of their activities.

Mitigation: Utilize file integrity monitoring tools to detect changes in file timestamps and identify potential tampering.

8.4.6 Cloud and Remote Infrastructure

Remote Infrastructure: Attackers may use compromised systems as jump points to launch attacks from other locations, making attribution more difficult.

Cloud-Based Attacks: Attackers may exploit cloud services to host malicious tools and exfiltrate data, making it harder to trace the attack's origin.

Mitigation: Monitor network traffic and implement network segmentation to limit lateral movement. Utilize cloud security best practices and conduct regular security assessments.

In conclusion, covering tracks and erasing evidence is a crucial part of an attacker's strategy to maintain stealth and avoid detection. Cybersecurity professionals must be proactive in detecting and mitigating potential cover-up techniques. Strong logging practices, centralized logging, endpoint security solutions, and incident response planning are essential for effectively countering attempts to erase evidence and enhance the chances of identifying and neutralizing ongoing threats.

Chapter 9: Forensics and Incident Response

Welcome to Chapter 9 of "The Kali Linux Handbook: A Practical Guide to Advanced Cybersecurity Techniques." In this critical chapter, we delve into the fascinating world of digital forensics and incident response—an indispensable skill set for investigating security incidents, analyzing digital evidence, and responding to cyber threats effectively.

Introduction to Digital Forensics

We begin by understanding the foundations of digital forensics—the process of collecting, preserving, and analyzing digital evidence from various sources. You'll learn the importance of maintaining the integrity of evidence and adhering to best practices in forensic investigations.

Preserving and Collecting Evidence

In this section, we explore the methods used to preserve and collect digital evidence, ensuring its admissibility in legal proceedings. From volatile data acquisition to imaging storage media, you'll learn how to handle evidence meticulously to maintain its probative value.

Analyzing Disk Images with Autopsy

Autopsy is a powerful open-source digital forensics tool widely used for analyzing disk images. In this part, we dive into Autopsy's features and capabilities, discovering how it simplifies the process of analyzing digital evidence. You'll learn how to conduct keyword searches, recover deleted files, and uncover hidden information to support your investigations.

Incident Response and Recovery

Incident response is a proactive approach to managing and responding to cybersecurity incidents promptly. In this final section, we explore the key steps involved in incident response, from detection and containment to eradication and recovery. By mastering incident response procedures, you'll be better prepared to mitigate the impact of security incidents and restore normal operations efficiently.

Throughout this chapter, we stress the ethical use of digital forensics and incident response techniques. These skills are essential not only for identifying and prosecuting cybercriminals but also for ensuring the resilience and continuity of organizations in the face of cyber threats.

By mastering digital forensics and incident response, you'll possess a vital skill set to protect your organization from potential cyber incidents and respond promptly and effectively when they occur.

Let's embrace the responsibilities of cybersecurity professionals and delve into the world of digital forensics and incident response, safeguarding the digital landscape and ensuring a secure and resilient future.

9.1 Introduction to Digital Forensics

Digital forensics, also known as computer forensics or cyber forensics, is a branch of forensic science that deals with the investigation and analysis of digital evidence to uncover and interpret information related to cybercrimes, security incidents, and other digital incidents. Digital forensics plays a crucial role in modern law enforcement, cybersecurity, and incident response efforts. It involves the collection, preservation, examination, analysis, and presentation of digital evidence in a manner that maintains its integrity and ensures it is admissible in a court of law. In this section, we will explore the basics of digital forensics and the key components involved in the investigative process.

9.1.1 The Role of Digital Forensics

Digital forensics is used to investigate a wide range of digital incidents, including:

Cybercrime Investigations: Digital forensics helps in identifying and prosecuting cybercriminals involved in activities such as hacking, data breaches, online fraud, and cyber-espionage.

Incident Response: In the aftermath of a security breach or cyber incident, digital forensics is used to determine the nature and scope of the attack, identify affected systems, and recover lost or compromised data.

Intellectual Property Theft: Digital forensics can assist in cases involving the theft of intellectual property, trade secrets, or proprietary information.

Employee Misconduct: When employee misconduct or insider threats are suspected, digital forensics can be used to analyze the employee's digital activities.

Electronic Discovery (eDiscovery): In legal cases, digital forensics is employed to identify, preserve, and analyze electronic evidence for use in court proceedings.

9.1.2 Key Components of Digital Forensics

Digital forensics investigations typically involve the following key components:

Evidence Collection: The first step is to identify and collect digital evidence, which may include data from computers, servers, mobile devices, cloud services, and network logs.

Evidence Preservation: Proper preservation of digital evidence is critical to maintaining its integrity and ensuring it is admissible in court. Forensic experts use specialized tools and procedures to create forensic images of storage media to avoid altering the original data.

Evidence Examination: Forensic analysts use various tools and techniques to examine the acquired data and identify relevant information. This may involve keyword searches, data carving (recovering deleted files), and data analysis.

Data Analysis: The examination of digital evidence may reveal patterns, timelines, and relationships that can help reconstruct events and identify potential suspects.

Reporting and Documentation: All findings and analysis must be documented in a detailed and comprehensive report that includes the methodology used, the evidence recovered, and the conclusions drawn.

Presentation in Court: In cases where digital evidence is presented in court, forensic experts may be required to testify as expert witnesses, explaining their findings and methodologies.

9.1.3 Challenges in Digital Forensics

Digital forensics investigations face several challenges:

Data Encryption: Encrypted data may be challenging to access without the necessary encryption keys or passwords.

Anti-Forensics Techniques: Attackers may employ anti-forensics techniques to hinder the investigation and cover their tracks.

Volume of Data: The sheer volume of digital data to analyze can be overwhelming, requiring efficient data processing and analysis techniques.

Legal and Privacy Concerns: Digital forensics must adhere to legal requirements and privacy regulations to ensure the admissibility of evidence in court.

Rapidly Evolving Technology: The continuous advancement of technology necessitates ongoing training and research for digital forensic experts to stay up-to-date with new tools and methodologies.

In conclusion, digital forensics is a crucial discipline for investigating cybercrimes and digital incidents. By following sound methodologies, preserving evidence integrity, and using specialized tools and techniques, digital forensics professionals play a critical role in unraveling complex digital mysteries and helping to uphold justice in the digital realm.

9.2 Preserving and Collecting Evidence

Preserving and collecting digital evidence is a critical aspect of digital forensics investigations. The proper handling of evidence ensures its integrity and admissibility in court, allowing investigators to reconstruct events accurately and identify potential suspects. Mishandling or neglecting to preserve evidence can lead to its contamination or loss, significantly compromising the investigation. In this section, we will explore the best practices for preserving and collecting digital evidence in digital forensics investigations.

9.2.1 Best Practices for Evidence Preservation

Document Everything: From the moment an incident is reported, meticulous documentation is essential. Record the date, time, location, and description of the evidence, as well as the names of individuals involved in the collection process.

Maintain Chain of Custody: Establish and maintain a clear chain of custody for the evidence. This involves documenting every individual who handles the evidence and the date and time of transfer between parties. This ensures that evidence remains tamper-free and admissible in court.

Limit Access: Restrict access to the evidence to authorized personnel only. This helps prevent accidental contamination or intentional tampering.

Make Forensic Copies: When collecting evidence from digital devices, create forensic copies (forensic images) of the original storage media using specialized tools. Forensic copies are read-only and ensure that the original data remains intact.

Hashing: Generate cryptographic hash values (such as MD5 or SHA-256) for the forensic copies. Hashes serve as digital fingerprints and help verify the integrity of the evidence throughout the investigation.

Store Evidence Securely: Physical evidence should be stored in a secure, climate-controlled environment to prevent damage, loss, or contamination. Digital evidence should be stored in encrypted storage to maintain confidentiality.

Preserve Metadata: Metadata (such as file creation dates, access times, and user information) is crucial in digital investigations. Ensure that metadata is preserved and included in the documentation.

9.2.2 Best Practices for Evidence Collection

Collect Volatile Data First: Volatile data, such as running processes, open network connections, and system logs, can be lost if the system is powered off. Collect this data first to capture real-time information.

Use Write-Blocking Devices: When collecting evidence from digital devices, use write-blocking devices or software to ensure that the original data is not altered during the collection process.

Physical Devices: If collecting physical devices (e.g., computers, smartphones), handle them carefully to avoid damaging or contaminating the evidence. Use appropriate anti-static precautions.

Network Data: For network-based evidence, use network capture tools (e.g., Wireshark) to capture packets and analyze network traffic related to the incident.

Document Connections and Locations: When dealing with network-based evidence, document IP addresses, ports, and network connections to understand the flow of data and potential communication with external entities.

Take Photographs: Document the physical setup of the crime scene or the location of digital devices through photographs. This can provide context and support the investigation.

Verify Integrity: After evidence collection, verify the integrity of the data by comparing the hash values of the forensic copies with the original hashes.

9.2.3 Legal Considerations

Digital forensics investigations must adhere to legal and regulatory requirements to ensure the admissibility of evidence in court. Important legal considerations include:

Search Warrants: In some cases, investigators may need search warrants before collecting evidence from certain devices or locations.

Data Privacy Laws: Ensure that the collection of digital evidence complies with data privacy laws and regulations governing the jurisdiction where the investigation is conducted.

Chain of Custody: As mentioned earlier, maintaining a clear chain of custody is crucial for legal admissibility. Any break in the chain of custody can weaken the evidence's credibility.

Expert Testimony: In court proceedings, forensic experts may be required to provide expert testimony to explain the methodologies used, the findings, and the significance of the evidence.

In conclusion, preserving and collecting digital evidence in a proper and systematic manner is vital for successful digital forensics investigations. Following best practices, adhering to legal requirements, and using specialized tools and techniques help ensure that evidence remains untainted and stands up to scrutiny in court. By conducting thorough and meticulous evidence preservation and collection, digital forensics professionals can aid in the pursuit of justice and the identification of those responsible for digital crimes and incidents.

9.3 Analyzing Disk Images with Autopsy

Autopsy is an open-source digital forensics tool widely used for analyzing disk images and conducting investigations in various cyber incidents. It provides a user-friendly graphical interface and a range of powerful features to assist digital forensics professionals in examining evidence and uncovering crucial information. In this section, we will explore the process of analyzing disk images with Autopsy and the key features it offers for conducting a thorough digital investigation.

9.3.1 Importing Disk Images

The first step in using Autopsy is to import the disk image or evidence file into the tool. Autopsy supports various disk image formats, including E01, DD, and AFF. To import a disk image, follow these steps:

Create a New Case: Launch Autopsy and create a new case for the investigation. The case stores all the evidence, reports, and analysis related to a specific investigation.

Add Evidence: In the case details, click on "Add Data Source" and select "Disk Image." Browse to the location of the disk image file and provide necessary details, such as the file format and password (if encrypted).

Indexing: Autopsy can optionally index the disk image to speed up searches and analysis. Indexing creates a searchable database of file metadata and content.

Start the Analysis: Once the disk image is added, Autopsy will start the analysis process, and the investigation can proceed.

9.3.2 Key Features of Autopsy

Autopsy provides a wide range of features for analyzing disk images and conducting digital investigations. Some of the key features include:

Keyword Search: Autopsy allows investigators to perform keyword searches on the disk image. This can help locate files, documents, or communication related to specific terms or subjects.

Timeline Analysis: The tool can create a timeline of events based on file timestamps, browser history, and other data. Timeline analysis aids in reconstructing the sequence of events during an incident.

File Carving: Autopsy can perform file carving to recover deleted or hidden files from the disk image. This feature is particularly useful when investigating data that has been intentionally or accidentally deleted.

Email Analysis: Autopsy can parse and analyze email artifacts, including email headers, bodies, and attachments, to reveal important communications.

Registry Analysis: The tool can examine Windows registry hives within the disk image, providing insights into system configuration, user activities, and software installations.

Hash Filtering: Autopsy supports hash filtering, which allows investigators to filter out known good files or known malicious files using hash databases.

Data Visualization: Autopsy provides various data visualization options, such as file type histograms, to help identify patterns and relationships in the evidence.

Reporting: The tool offers comprehensive reporting capabilities, allowing investigators to generate detailed reports summarizing their findings and analysis.

Keyword Lists: Investigators can create and use custom keyword lists to facilitate targeted searches and highlight specific types of evidence.

9.3.3 Analyzing Disk Images Step-by-Step

The process of analyzing disk images with Autopsy can be summarized in the following steps:

Import Disk Image: Create a new case, add the disk image as the data source, and configure the necessary settings.

Start Analysis: Allow Autopsy to process and analyze the disk image to index the data and prepare it for investigation.

Keyword Search: Use keyword searches to locate relevant files or information related to the investigation.

Timeline Analysis: Create a timeline to visualize events and activities on the system over time.

File Carving: Perform file carving to recover deleted files or data fragments that may be relevant to the investigation.

Email and Registry Analysis: Examine email artifacts and registry entries for valuable information.

Data Visualization: Utilize data visualization tools to identify patterns and trends in the evidence.

Hash Filtering: Apply hash filters to exclude known good files or known malicious files from the investigation.

Generate Reports: Generate comprehensive reports summarizing the investigation's findings and analysis.

9.3.4 Legal Considerations

When using Autopsy or any other digital forensics tool, investigators must ensure that they adhere to legal and regulatory requirements. Legal considerations for digital investigations include:

Warrants and Authorization: Ensure that proper legal authorization, such as search warrants or consent, is obtained before analyzing disk images.

Chain of Custody: Maintain a clear chain of custody for the evidence, ensuring it is properly documented and secured throughout the investigation.

Data Privacy and Confidentiality: Respect data privacy laws and handle sensitive or confidential information appropriately.

Expert Testimony: Be prepared to provide expert testimony in court, explaining the methods used, the findings, and the significance of the evidence.

In conclusion, Autopsy is a powerful digital forensics tool for analyzing disk images and conducting investigations. Its user-friendly interface and comprehensive features make it a valuable asset for digital forensics professionals. By following best practices, adhering to legal requirements, and utilizing the capabilities of Autopsy effectively, investigators can conduct thorough and successful digital investigations and contribute to the pursuit of justice in the digital realm.

9.4 Incident Response and Recovery

Incident response is a critical aspect of digital forensics that focuses on detecting, responding to, and recovering from cybersecurity incidents and data breaches. When an incident occurs, such as a security breach, malware infection, or unauthorized access, an effective incident response plan is crucial to minimize the impact, contain the threat, and restore normal operations. In this section, we will explore the key components of incident response and recovery in digital forensics.

9.4.1 Incident Response Lifecycle

The incident response lifecycle consists of several key phases:

Preparation: This phase involves proactively preparing for potential incidents by establishing an incident response team, defining roles and responsibilities, and creating an incident response plan.

Identification: The identification phase involves detecting and recognizing the signs of an incident. This may include the analysis of system logs, network traffic, and security alerts.

Containment: Once an incident is identified, the primary focus is to contain the threat and prevent further damage. This may involve isolating affected systems, blocking malicious traffic, or shutting down compromised services.

Eradication: After containment, the next step is to remove the cause of the incident. This may involve removing malware, patching vulnerabilities, or reconfiguring security settings.

Recovery: The recovery phase focuses on restoring affected systems and services to normal operation. This may involve data restoration from backups or rebuilding compromised systems.

Lessons Learned: After the incident is resolved, the incident response team conducts a post-incident review to identify lessons learned and areas for improvement in the incident response process.

9.4.2 Role of Digital Forensics in Incident Response

Digital forensics plays a crucial role in incident response:

Evidence Collection: Digital forensics experts collect and preserve evidence related to the incident. This includes disk images, memory snapshots, network logs, and other artifacts that may be used for further analysis and investigation.

Investigation and Analysis: Forensic experts analyze the collected evidence to identify the root cause of the incident, the extent of the damage, and the techniques used by the attackers.

Malware Analysis: If malware is involved in the incident, digital forensics experts conduct malware analysis to understand its behavior and capabilities.

Attribution and Threat Intelligence: Digital forensics can provide valuable information for attributing the attack to specific threat actors and help improve threat intelligence to prevent similar incidents in the future.

9.4.3 Digital Forensics in Recovery

Digital forensics also plays a role in the recovery phase of incident response:

Data Recovery: Digital forensics experts assist in recovering lost or corrupted data, either from backups or through data carving techniques to reconstruct files.

System Restoration: Forensic experts help restore affected systems to a known good state, ensuring that they are free from any lingering threats.

Security Improvements: The findings from the digital forensics investigation may lead to security improvements, such as patching vulnerabilities or implementing additional security controls.

9.4.4 Incident Response and Legal Considerations

During incident response and recovery, legal considerations are paramount:

Chain of Custody: Properly maintain the chain of custody for all evidence collected during the incident response process to ensure its admissibility in legal proceedings.

Data Privacy and Compliance: Adhere to data privacy laws and regulations while collecting, analyzing, and sharing data related to the incident.

Legal Obligations: Understand and fulfill any legal obligations regarding incident reporting, disclosure to stakeholders, or law enforcement involvement.

Expert Testimony: Be prepared to provide expert testimony in court if the incident leads to legal proceedings.

9.4.5 Continuous Improvement

After resolving an incident, it is crucial to conduct a thorough post-incident review and update the incident response plan accordingly. Continuous improvement helps organizations better prepare for future incidents and enhance their incident response capabilities.

In conclusion, incident response and recovery are essential components of digital forensics that help organizations effectively respond to cybersecurity incidents and mitigate their impact. Digital forensics experts play a critical role in identifying the cause of incidents, collecting evidence, and assisting in the recovery process. By following a well-defined incident response plan, adhering to legal considerations, and conducting post-incident reviews, organizations can strengthen their incident response capabilities and better protect themselves from future threats.

Chapter 10: Advanced Kali Linux Tools

Welcome to Chapter 10 of "The Kali Linux Handbook: A Practical Guide to Advanced Cybersecurity Techniques." In this chapter, we embark on an exciting exploration of advanced Kali Linux tools—powerful cybersecurity utilities that go beyond the basics, empowering you to tackle complex security challenges with finesse.

Harnessing the Power of Nmap NSE

Nmap (Network Mapper) is a versatile and essential tool for network exploration and security auditing. In this section, we take a deep dive into Nmap's scripting engine (NSE), a feature that extends Nmap's capabilities with custom scripts. You'll learn how to leverage NSE scripts to automate advanced scanning, gather more targeted information, and enhance your network assessments.

Exploiting Web Vulnerabilities with Burp Suite

Burp Suite is a widely used and robust web application security testing tool. In this part, we explore the various components of Burp Suite, including its Proxy, Scanner, and Intruder modules. You'll learn how to identify and exploit web vulnerabilities, such as Cross-Site Scripting (XSS) and SQL injection, to bolster your web application security assessments.

Cracking Passwords with Hashcat

Hashcat is a powerful password cracking tool, renowned for its efficiency and speed. In this section, we delve into the art of password cracking using Hashcat's GPU acceleration capabilities. You'll understand various password hashing algorithms and how to crack passwords from captured hashes, emphasizing the importance of strong and secure password practices.

Analyzing Wireless Networks with Aircrack-ng

Aircrack-ng is a collection of tools used for wireless network security assessments. In this final section, we explore the capabilities of Aircrack-ng, from capturing wireless packets to cracking WPA/WPA2 encrypted networks. You'll learn how to analyze and evaluate the security of wireless networks effectively, helping organizations safeguard their wireless communications.

Throughout this chapter, we stress the responsible and ethical use of advanced Kali Linux tools. These powerful utilities are essential assets in the hands of cybersecurity professionals, enabling proactive assessments and improved security postures.

By mastering advanced Kali Linux tools, you'll possess formidable skillset to tackle complex cybersecurity challenges head-on. Let's embrace the power of Kali Linux and harness these advanced tools to fortify our organization's defenses and safeguard the digital world.

10.1 Harnessing the Power of Nmap NSE

Nmap (Network Mapper) is a powerful and widely used open-source network scanning tool that allows cybersecurity professionals to discover hosts and services on a computer network, thus creating a "map" of the network's topology. Nmap's real strength lies in its extensibility through the Nmap Scripting Engine (NSE). The NSE enables users to write and execute custom scripts to perform a wide range of network-related tasks, making Nmap a versatile tool for advanced network scanning and analysis. In this section, we will explore the capabilities of Nmap NSE and how it can be harnessed to enhance network security assessments.

10.1.1 Understanding Nmap NSE

The Nmap Scripting Engine (NSE) is a flexible and powerful feature that extends Nmap's functionality beyond its built-in capabilities. NSE scripts are written in the Lua programming language and can perform various tasks, including service version detection, vulnerability scanning, brute-force attacks, and network discovery. Nmap comes with a significant number of pre-built scripts, and users can also create their own custom scripts to tailor the scanning process to their specific needs.

10.1.2 Key Features and Use Cases of Nmap NSE

Service Version Detection: Nmap NSE scripts can identify the versions of services running on open ports. This information is valuable for understanding potential vulnerabilities associated with specific service versions.

Vulnerability Scanning: NSE scripts can be used to detect known vulnerabilities in network services and applications. This helps in identifying potential weaknesses that may be exploited by attackers.

Brute-Force Attacks: NSE scripts can perform brute-force attacks against services that require authentication, helping assess the strength of passwords and authentication mechanisms.

Network Discovery: Nmap NSE can be used for network discovery tasks, such as finding live hosts, detecting open ports, and identifying services running on those ports.

Network Enumeration: NSE scripts can enumerate network information, such as user accounts, shares, and resources, to gain a deeper understanding of the target environment.

Integration with Other Tools: Nmap NSE can be combined with other security tools and frameworks to create comprehensive security assessments.

10.1.3 Running NSE Scripts with Nmap

To use NSE scripts with Nmap, the -sC option is used along with the desired script category. For example, to run default scripts, the command would be:

nmap -sC target_ip

To specify individual NSE scripts, the --script option is used:

nmap --script script_name target_ip

To run all available NSE scripts against a target, use:

nmap -sC -sV -p- target_ip

The -sV option enables version detection, and -p- tells Nmap to scan all 65535 ports.

10.1.4 Customizing NSE Scripts

Users can customize NSE scripts to suit their specific requirements. This involves modifying existing scripts or writing new ones in Lua. The NSE scripts are stored in the "scripts" directory of the Nmap installation. By default, Nmap looks for scripts in this directory, but users can specify additional script directories using the --script-path option.

When customizing scripts, it is essential to understand the Lua programming language and the Nmap NSE API, which provides functions and libraries to interact with Nmap's scanning engine and access scan results.

10.1.5 Best Practices and Security Considerations

While Nmap NSE is a powerful tool, it should be used responsibly and ethically. Some best practices and security considerations when using Nmap NSE include:

Permission and Authorization: Always obtain proper permission and authorization before scanning networks. Unauthorized scanning is illegal and unethical.

Minimize Impact: NSE scripts can be resource-intensive and cause network disruptions. Use targeted scanning and consider the impact on network performance.

Vulnerability Testing: When conducting vulnerability scanning, ensure that it is performed against systems and networks under your control or with explicit authorization.

Keep Scripts Updated: Regularly update NSE scripts to ensure they are current and capable of detecting the latest vulnerabilities.

Review Script Output: Carefully review the output of NSE scripts to avoid misinterpretation or false positives.

Log and Document: Maintain detailed logs and documentation of the scanning process, including the purpose, scope, and results.

10.1.6 Community and Script Sharing

The Nmap scripting community is active and constantly contributing new scripts and updates. Users can explore the Nmap Scripting Database (https://nmap.org/nsedoc/) to discover available scripts and their descriptions. Additionally, users can share their custom scripts with the community, fostering collaboration and improving the capabilities of Nmap NSE.

In conclusion, Nmap NSE is a powerful extension of the Nmap network scanning tool, providing users with the ability to perform advanced network scanning, vulnerability assessment, and network discovery tasks. By leveraging the capabilities of Nmap NSE responsibly and adhering to best practices and security considerations, cybersecurity professionals can enhance their network security assessments and gain valuable insights into potential risks and vulnerabilities within their networks.

10.2 Exploiting Web Vulnerabilities with Burp Suite

Burp Suite is a popular and powerful web application security testing tool used by cybersecurity professionals to discover and exploit web application vulnerabilities. It offers a comprehensive set of features and functionalities that aid in the identification, analysis, and exploitation of security flaws in web applications. In this section, we will explore how Burp Suite can be utilized to exploit web vulnerabilities and assess the security of web applications.

10.2.1 Understanding Burp Suite

Burp Suite is an integrated platform developed by PortSwigger for web application security testing. It consists of several modules, including:

Proxy: The Proxy module acts as a web proxy server, intercepting and inspecting HTTP/HTTPS traffic between the user's browser and the target web application. This enables users to view and modify requests and responses, making it an essential tool for manual testing and exploitation.

Scanner: The Scanner module automates the process of identifying common web application vulnerabilities, such as SQL injection, cross-site scripting (XSS), and others. It scans the target web application for potential security flaws and provides detailed vulnerability reports.

Intruder: The Intruder module is used for performing automated and manual web application attacks, such as brute-force attacks, parameter fuzzing, and more. It helps identify vulnerabilities that require repetitive or iterative testing.

Repeater: The Repeater module allows users to modify and reissue individual HTTP requests to the web application. This is useful for testing how the application responds to different inputs and payloads.

Sequencer: The Sequencer module analyzes the randomness and quality of session tokens or other random data used in web applications, helping to identify weaknesses in their generation.

Decoder: The Decoder module provides tools to encode or decode data in various formats, making it useful for understanding how data is processed and transmitted in web applications.

10.2.2 Identifying Web Vulnerabilities

Before exploiting web vulnerabilities, it is essential to identify them. Burp Suite's Scanner module can be used to automatically scan the web application for common vulnerabilities. The process involves configuring the target scope, initiating the scan, and reviewing the vulnerability findings. However, it is important to note that automated scanning may not always identify all vulnerabilities, and manual testing is often required for comprehensive assessment.

Manual vulnerability identification involves using the Proxy module to intercept and modify requests, testing for security flaws like XSS, SQL injection, path traversal, and more. The Intruder module can be employed to perform parameter fuzzing and brute-force attacks to identify weaknesses in input validation and authentication mechanisms.

10.2.3 Exploiting Web Vulnerabilities

Once vulnerabilities are identified, Burp Suite can be used to exploit them to understand their impact and demonstrate their potential risk to the application and its data. For example:

SQL Injection: Using the SQL injection vulnerability, an attacker can modify SQL queries to extract or manipulate the application's database, potentially accessing sensitive data.

Cross-Site Scripting (XSS): Exploiting XSS allows an attacker to inject malicious scripts into web pages, stealing cookies, session tokens, or redirecting users to malicious sites.

Path Traversal: By exploiting path traversal vulnerabilities, an attacker can access files and directories outside the application's intended scope.

Command Injection: Command injection allows attackers to execute arbitrary system commands on the web server.

The Burp Suite Intruder module is particularly useful for automating the exploitation process, as it can be configured to perform a large number of requests with different payloads, parameters, and combinations. This helps in identifying the extent of the vulnerability and its impact on the application.

10.2.4 Responsible and Ethical Use

It is crucial to emphasize that Burp Suite or any other web application security tool should only be used on systems and applications for which you have explicit authorization. Unauthorized scanning and exploitation of web applications are illegal and unethical and can lead to severe consequences.

Ethical hackers and cybersecurity professionals should follow responsible disclosure practices, reporting the identified vulnerabilities to the application owner or administrator promptly and responsibly. This allows the organization to fix the vulnerabilities before they can be exploited maliciously.

10.2.5 Continuous Web Application Security Testing

Web application security testing is an ongoing process. As web applications evolve and change over time, new vulnerabilities may arise. Regular security testing with tools like Burp Suite ensures that web applications remain secure and protected against emerging threats.

In conclusion, Burp Suite is a powerful tool for web application security testing and vulnerability exploitation. By using its various modules responsibly and following ethical practices, cybersecurity professionals can identify and demonstrate web application vulnerabilities, helping organizations enhance their security posture and protect against potential attacks.

10.3 Cracking Passwords with Hashcat

Hashcat is a popular and powerful open-source password cracking tool used by cybersecurity professionals and ethical hackers to recover lost or forgotten passwords from hashed data. It is capable of performing high-speed password cracking using various attack modes and techniques. In this section, we will explore how Hashcat can be utilized to crack passwords from hashed data and the considerations that must be taken into account when using this tool.

10.3.1 Understanding Password Hashing

Password hashing is a process used to convert plain-text passwords into irreversible cryptographic representations called hashes. When a user creates an account or sets a password, the password is hashed and stored in the system's database. During the authentication process, the user's entered password is hashed again, and the result is compared with the stored hash. If the two hashes match, the user is granted access.

Hash functions used for password hashing are designed to be one-way and non-reversible. This means that it is computationally infeasible to convert the hash back into the original plain-text password. The security of password hashing lies in this irreversibility, as it makes it challenging for attackers to obtain the actual passwords from the hashes.

10.3.2 Cracking Passwords with Hashcat

Hashcat is capable of cracking passwords from hashed data through various attack modes:

Dictionary Attack: In a dictionary attack, Hashcat uses a wordlist (dictionary) containing a list of common passwords, phrases, and variations. It hashes each word and compares the generated hashes with the target hash. If a match is found, the original password is considered cracked.

Brute-Force Attack: In a brute-force attack, Hashcat systematically tries every possible combination of characters within a specified length range. This method is time-consuming but can eventually crack even complex passwords.

Mask Attack: A mask attack allows users to define a custom password pattern using placeholders for characters such as uppercase letters, lowercase letters, digits, and special symbols.

Rule-Based Attack: A rule-based attack applies various transformations to the words in the dictionary, such as appending numbers or capitalizing letters, to increase the chances of cracking complex passwords.

10.3.3 Preparing Hashes for Cracking

Before using Hashcat to crack passwords, the hashes must be extracted from the target system or application. Hashes can be found in various places, such as the /etc/shadow file on Linux systems or the SAM registry hive on Windows systems.

Hashcat supports a wide range of hash types, including MD5, SHA1, SHA256, bcrypt, and more. It is essential to specify the correct hash type during the cracking process, as each hash type requires a different approach and processing time.

10.3.4 Best Practices and Legal Considerations

Cracking passwords with Hashcat can be resource-intensive and time-consuming, especially for complex passwords. Ethical hackers and cybersecurity professionals should follow these best practices and legal considerations:

Authorization: Ensure that you have explicit authorization from the system or application owner to perform password cracking. Unauthorized password cracking is illegal and unethical.

Responsible Use: Only crack passwords for which you have a legitimate reason and authorization. Avoid cracking passwords for personal gain or without a valid purpose.

Password Complexity: Encourage users to choose strong and complex passwords to make cracking attempts more challenging.

Hashcat Performance: Optimize Hashcat's performance by using GPUs or specialized hardware for faster password cracking.

Secure Hash Storage: Store password hashes securely to prevent unauthorized access to the hashed passwords.

Post-Cracking Actions: If you successfully crack passwords, use this information responsibly and ensure that the passwords are changed and notified to users.

10.3.5 Continuous Password Security

Password security is an ongoing process. Organizations should regularly update their password policies, enforce password complexity rules, and educate users about secure password practices. Additionally, using modern and strong password hashing algorithms like bcrypt or Argon2 is crucial to enhance password security and make password cracking attempts more challenging.

In conclusion, Hashcat is a powerful tool used for password cracking and is essential for ethical hackers and cybersecurity professionals to assess the strength of passwords and improve overall password security. However, it is crucial to use Hashcat responsibly, with proper authorization, and in compliance with legal and ethical considerations to maintain the integrity of the cybersecurity profession.

10.4 Analyzing Wireless Networks with Aircrack-ng

Aircrack-ng is a popular and powerful suite of tools used by cybersecurity professionals and ethical hackers for analyzing and assessing the security of wireless networks. It provides a range of capabilities for capturing, analyzing, and cracking wireless network encryption keys, making it a valuable tool for wireless network security assessments. In this section, we will explore how Aircrack-ng can be utilized to analyze wireless networks and the considerations that must be taken into account when using this tool.

10.4.1 Understanding Wireless Network Security

Wireless networks use encryption to protect data transmitted over the airwaves. The most common wireless security protocols are WEP (Wired Equivalent Privacy), WPA (Wi-Fi Protected Access), and WPA2. However, some older networks may still use the outdated and insecure WEP protocol.

Aircrack-ng is primarily used to assess the security of WEP and WPA/WPA2-PSK (Pre-Shared Key) encrypted networks. It works by capturing packets from the wireless network and attempting to crack the encryption key through various methods.

10.4.2 Capturing Packets with Airodump-ng

The first step in analyzing a wireless network with Aircrack-ng is to capture packets from the target network using the Airodump-ng tool. Airodump-ng is a network packet capture tool that captures 802.11 wireless frames from the air and saves them to a file for further analysis.

To capture packets, use the following command:

airodump-ng <interface>

Replace <interface> with the name of the wireless network interface in monitor mode. Airodump-ng will start scanning for nearby wireless networks and display information about the networks it finds, including their BSSID (MAC address), channel, and encryption type.

10.4.3 Cracking WEP Encryption

For WEP-encrypted networks, Aircrack-ng can be used to crack the encryption key by analyzing the captured packets. WEP is weak and vulnerable to various attacks, such as the FMS attack and the PTW attack, which Aircrack-ng supports.

To crack WEP encryption, use the following command:

aircrack-ng -b <BSSID> -w <wordlist> <capture-file.cap>

Replace <BSSID> with the MAC address of the target network, <wordlist> with the path to a wordlist file containing potential WEP keys, and <capture-file.cap> with the name of the captured packet file.

Aircrack-ng will start the cracking process and attempt to find the WEP key in the wordlist. If the correct key is present in the wordlist, Aircrack-ng will successfully crack the WEP encryption.

10.4.4 Cracking WPA/WPA2-PSK Encryption

Cracking WPA/WPA2-PSK encryption is more challenging than WEP and may require significantly more time and computational resources. Aircrack-ng uses a dictionary attack against the pre-shared key to attempt to crack WPA/WPA2-PSK.

To crack WPA/WPA2-PSK encryption, use the following command:

aircrack-ng -b <BSSID> -w <wordlist> <capture-file.cap>

Replace <BSSID> with the MAC address of the target network, <wordlist> with the path to a wordlist file containing potential passwords, and <capture-file.cap> with the name of the captured packet file.

Aircrack-ng will start the dictionary attack, trying each password in the wordlist until it finds the correct one. Successful cracking depends on the strength of the password and the size and quality of the wordlist.

10.4.5 Legal and Ethical Considerations

Using Aircrack-ng to analyze and assess the security of wireless networks raises important legal and ethical considerations:

Authorization: Only use Aircrack-ng on wireless networks for which you have explicit authorization. Unauthorized network scanning and cracking are illegal and unethical.

Own or Authorized Networks: Limit Aircrack-ng usage to your own networks or networks for which you have been granted permission to perform security assessments.

Privacy and Data Protection: Be aware of the potential for capturing sensitive data during network analysis and ensure that privacy and data protection laws are adhered to.

Responsible Disclosure: If vulnerabilities or weaknesses are identified during the assessment, responsibly disclose the findings to the network owner or administrator.

10.4.6 Continuous Network Security

Wireless network security is an ongoing process. Regularly update the Wi-Fi encryption protocol to WPA3, which is the most secure and robust encryption standard currently available. Additionally, enforce strong password policies and conduct regular security assessments to identify and address potential weaknesses in wireless networks.

In conclusion, Aircrack-ng is a powerful tool for analyzing wireless network security and assessing the effectiveness of encryption mechanisms. However, it must be used responsibly, with proper authorization, and in compliance with legal and ethical considerations to maintain the integrity of the cybersecurity profession.

Chapter 11: Kali Linux for IoT and Embedded Systems

Welcome to Chapter 11 of "The Kali Linux Handbook: A Practical Guide to Advanced Cybersecurity Techniques." In this chapter, we delve into the dynamic world of Internet of Things (IoT) and Embedded Systems, exploring how Kali Linux can be leveraged to assess the security of these interconnected devices.

Understanding IoT Security Challenges

We begin by examining the unique security challenges presented by the Internet of Things. As IoT devices proliferate in our homes, workplaces, and industries, they become attractive targets for cyber attackers. In this section, we explore the vulnerabilities and risks associated with IoT deployments, setting the stage for our assessments.

Assessing IoT Device Vulnerabilities

In this part, we dive into the process of assessing IoT devices for security weaknesses. We'll explore the methodologies and tools used to discover vulnerabilities, such as insecure configurations, default credentials, and outdated firmware. By understanding these weaknesses, you'll be equipped to identify and address IoT device security risks.

Exploiting Embedded Systems

Embedded systems are at the heart of IoT devices, and understanding their vulnerabilities is crucial for assessing overall IoT security. In this section, we explore techniques for exploiting vulnerabilities in embedded systems, such as buffer overflows and code injection. You'll gain insights into the tactics used by attackers to compromise these critical components.

Securing IoT Devices with Kali Linux

In this final section, we shift our focus to the proactive side of IoT security. You'll learn how to use Kali Linux tools to secure IoT devices and strengthen their resilience against potential attacks. From implementing secure communication protocols to configuring access controls, you'll be equipped to safeguard IoT deployments effectively.

Throughout this chapter, we stress the importance of responsible IoT security practices. With the growing prevalence of IoT devices in our lives, it is vital to ensure they are secure, protecting user privacy and critical infrastructure.

By mastering Kali Linux for IoT and Embedded Systems, you'll be at the forefront of securing this rapidly evolving technology landscape. Let's harness the power of Kali Linux to bolster IoT security and pave the way for a safer and more connected future.

11.1 Understanding IoT Security Challenges

The Internet of Things (IoT) has rapidly transformed the way we interact with technology, connecting everyday devices and objects to the internet and each other. While IoT offers numerous benefits and conveniences, it also introduces a wide range of security challenges. IoT devices often have limited resources and capabilities, making them vulnerable targets for cyberattacks. In this section, we will explore the significant security challenges associated with IoT and the potential risks they pose.

11.1.1 Proliferation of IoT Devices

The proliferation of IoT devices has created a massive attack surface for cybercriminals. These devices are embedded in various environments, from smart homes and industrial systems to healthcare and transportation. The sheer number and diversity of IoT devices make it challenging to implement consistent security measures across the entire IoT ecosystem.

11.1.2 Weak Authentication and Authorization

Many IoT devices come with default or weak credentials, such as default usernames and passwords. Additionally, some devices lack robust authentication and authorization mechanisms, making it easier for attackers to gain unauthorized access. Weak or default credentials are a common entry point for cyberattacks, leading to device compromise and potential data breaches.

11.1.3 Lack of Encryption

Data transmitted between IoT devices and backend systems is often not adequately encrypted, leaving it vulnerable to interception and tampering. Without proper encryption, sensitive information, including personal data, can be exposed to eavesdroppers, leading to privacy violations and potential misuse.

11.1.4 Firmware Vulnerabilities

IoT devices are commonly built on firmware, and manufacturers may not prioritize regular firmware updates or security patches. This leaves devices susceptible to known vulnerabilities that can be exploited by attackers to gain control over the devices or compromise the entire IoT network.

11.1.5 Insecure Communication Protocols

IoT devices often use various communication protocols, some of which may lack robust security features. Protocols like Zigbee, Bluetooth, and MQTT might not provide adequate protection against interception, replay attacks, or man-in-the-middle attacks, leaving the communication channel vulnerable to exploitation.

11.1.6 Physical Security

Many IoT devices are deployed in physically accessible environments, such as smart home devices and industrial sensors. Physical access to these devices can lead to tampering, unauthorized modifications, or direct attacks on the hardware.

11.1.7 Lack of Standardization

The lack of standardization in IoT security practices and protocols makes it challenging to establish consistent security standards across different devices and manufacturers. This lack of uniformity can lead to security gaps and inconsistencies in the implementation of security measures.

11.1.8 Supply Chain Risks

The global nature of IoT supply chains can introduce risks, such as compromised components or software being integrated into IoT devices during the manufacturing process. Attackers could exploit these vulnerabilities to compromise devices before they even reach end-users.

11.1.9 Distributed Denial of Service (DDoS) Attacks

IoT devices can be harnessed by attackers to participate in large-scale DDoS attacks. By compromising a vast network of insecure IoT devices, known as a botnet, attackers can overwhelm websites and online services with massive amounts of traffic, causing service disruptions.

11.1.10 Lack of User Awareness

End-users may not be fully aware of the security risks associated with IoT devices, leading to poor security practices such as not changing default passwords, neglecting firmware updates, or failing to secure their home networks properly.

11.1.11 Regulatory and Compliance Challenges

Regulatory frameworks and standards for IoT security are still evolving, making it challenging for manufacturers and users to adhere to specific security requirements. This lack of clear guidelines can hinder the adoption of robust security practices.

In conclusion, IoT security challenges stem from the vast and diverse landscape of interconnected devices, combined with the limited resources and capabilities of these devices. Addressing these challenges requires a collaborative effort from manufacturers, developers, users, and policymakers to implement strong security measures, raise awareness, and establish comprehensive regulatory frameworks. By prioritizing IoT security, we can better protect against cyber threats and ensure the safe and reliable deployment of IoT technologies in various domains.

11.2 Assessing IoT Device Vulnerabilities

Assessing the vulnerabilities of IoT devices is a crucial step in identifying potential security weaknesses and mitigating cyber risks. Due to the unique characteristics of IoT devices, traditional security assessment approaches may not be sufficient. In this section, we will explore the methods and best practices for assessing IoT device vulnerabilities effectively.

11.2.1 Threat Modeling

Threat modeling is the process of identifying and evaluating potential threats and risks associated with IoT devices. It involves understanding the device's architecture, components, communication channels, and potential attack vectors. By creating a threat model, security professionals can prioritize security measures based on the most significant threats to the device and its ecosystem.

11.2.2 Penetration Testing

Penetration testing, also known as ethical hacking, involves simulating real-world attacks on IoT devices to identify vulnerabilities and weaknesses. Penetration testers use various tools and techniques to assess the device's security posture and attempt to exploit potential vulnerabilities. It is essential to perform penetration testing in a controlled environment to avoid unintended consequences.

11.2.3 Firmware Analysis

Analyzing the firmware of an IoT device is critical for uncovering potential vulnerabilities and understanding its security mechanisms. Security researchers can use reverse engineering techniques to analyze the firmware and identify any exposed sensitive information, hardcoded credentials, or insecure coding practices.

11.2.4 Code Review

Performing a code review is an essential step to identify security flaws in the software running on the IoT device. This involves examining the device's source code for vulnerabilities, potential buffer overflows, injection vulnerabilities, or other coding errors that could lead to security breaches.

11.2.5 Radio Frequency (RF) Analysis

IoT devices often communicate wirelessly, making them susceptible to radio frequency attacks. RF analysis involves monitoring the wireless communication between IoT devices and identifying potential weaknesses in encryption, authentication, and data integrity.

11.2.6 Physical Security Assessment

Assessing the physical security of IoT devices is crucial, especially for devices deployed in uncontrolled environments. Physical security assessments involve evaluating the device's resistance to tampering, reverse engineering, or unauthorized access.

11.2.7 Supply Chain Assessment

The supply chain of IoT devices can introduce vulnerabilities if not properly secured. Assessing the supply chain involves ensuring that all components and software integrated into the devices are from trusted sources and have not been compromised during production or distribution.

11.2.8 Third-Party Component Analysis

Many IoT devices use third-party components, libraries, and modules in their software. It is crucial to assess the security of these components to avoid potential vulnerabilities inherited from third-party sources.

11.2.9 Network Security Assessment

IoT devices are part of larger ecosystems, and their security is closely tied to the security of the networks they connect to. Assessing network security involves evaluating the network architecture, access controls, and communication protocols to ensure that IoT devices are protected from network-based attacks.

11.2.10 Vulnerability Scanning

Automated vulnerability scanning tools can be used to quickly identify common vulnerabilities in IoT devices. These tools can scan the device's firmware, ports, and services to identify potential security flaws.

11.2.11 Secure Development Lifecycle (SDL) Review

A review of the device's development lifecycle can provide insights into the security practices followed during the development process. A well-defined Secure Development Lifecycle (SDL) can help prevent security issues from being introduced during the development phase.

In conclusion, assessing IoT device vulnerabilities is a multifaceted process that requires a combination of technical expertise, analysis, and testing. It involves evaluating the device's hardware, firmware, software, communication channels, and surrounding ecosystem. By conducting comprehensive security assessments and adopting a proactive approach to security, IoT device manufacturers and developers can enhance the overall security of IoT devices and protect against potential cyber threats.

11.3 Exploiting Embedded Systems

Embedded systems are specialized computing devices designed for specific tasks or functions, such as those found in IoT devices, industrial control systems, medical devices, automotive systems, and more. These systems often have limited resources and may run on custom operating systems or firmware. Exploiting embedded systems can lead to significant security risks and potential consequences. In this section, we will explore the methods and techniques used to exploit embedded systems and the importance of securing them against cyber threats.

11.3.1 Identifying Vulnerabilities

The first step in exploiting an embedded system is identifying vulnerabilities. Vulnerabilities can exist in the underlying operating system, firmware, applications, or communication protocols. Common vulnerabilities include buffer overflows, code injection, privilege escalation, insecure default configurations, and weak authentication mechanisms.

Vulnerability discovery can be achieved through various means, including manual code review, firmware analysis, reverse engineering, network scanning, and security testing using tools like fuzzers to identify potential software weaknesses.

11.3.2 Reverse Engineering

Reverse engineering is a critical technique used to understand the inner workings of embedded systems. By analyzing the device's firmware or software, security researchers can gain insights into its logic, communication protocols, and potential weak points. Reverse engineering helps identify exploitable vulnerabilities, hardcoded credentials, and undocumented functionality that may pose security risks.

11.3.3 Firmware Exploitation

Many embedded systems run on firmware, making them susceptible to firmware exploitation. Attackers can attempt to extract, modify, or replace the firmware to gain unauthorized access or control over the device. This can be achieved through techniques such as firmware dumping, analysis, modification, and re-flashing.

11.3.4 Exploiting Network Protocols

Embedded systems often communicate with other devices or backend systems over networks. Attackers can attempt to exploit network protocols to intercept, manipulate, or spoof communications. Vulnerable network protocols may allow attackers to perform man-in-the-middle attacks, packet injection, or denial-of-service (DoS) attacks.

11.3.5 Physical Attacks

Physical access to embedded systems can provide attackers with significant advantages. Physical attacks can involve tampering with the device, extracting sensitive data, or extracting firmware for analysis. Secure boot mechanisms, tamper-resistant hardware, and physical protection are essential in mitigating physical attacks.

11.3.6 Exploiting Default Credentials

Embedded systems sometimes come with default credentials for administrative access. Attackers can attempt to exploit these default credentials to gain unauthorized access to the system. It is crucial to change default credentials during device setup to prevent such attacks.

11.3.7 Injection Attacks

Injection attacks, such as code injection or command injection, are common techniques used to exploit vulnerable embedded systems. Attackers can inject malicious code or commands into the system to gain control or access sensitive data.

11.3.8 Buffer Overflows

Buffer overflow vulnerabilities can be exploited to overwrite memory areas beyond the intended boundaries, leading to potential code execution or system crashes. Proper input validation and boundary checks are critical to prevent buffer overflow exploits.

11.3.9 Privilege Escalation

Privilege escalation exploits involve gaining higher levels of access than intended by the device's design. Attackers can exploit privilege escalation vulnerabilities to gain administrative or root access, which can lead to complete control over the system.

11.3.10 Protecting Embedded Systems

To protect embedded systems from exploitation, the following security measures should be implemented:

Secure Development Practices: Adhere to secure coding practices and follow a secure development lifecycle (SDL) to reduce the likelihood of introducing vulnerabilities during the development process.

Firmware and Software Updates: Regularly update firmware and software to patch known vulnerabilities and strengthen the security of the embedded system.

Secure Boot and Hardware Protections: Implement secure boot mechanisms and hardware protections to prevent unauthorized firmware modifications and physical attacks.

Vulnerability Assessments and Penetration Testing: Conduct regular security assessments, vulnerability assessments, and penetration testing to identify and address potential weaknesses.

Network Security: Secure communication channels and protocols to prevent unauthorized access and data interception.

Authentication and Authorization: Implement strong authentication and authorization mechanisms to prevent unauthorized access to the device.

Monitoring and Intrusion Detection: Implement monitoring and intrusion detection systems to detect unusual or suspicious activities on the embedded system.

In conclusion, exploiting embedded systems can lead to severe security risks and consequences. Identifying vulnerabilities, securing the development process, and implementing robust security measures are crucial steps in protecting embedded systems from exploitation. By prioritizing security from the design stage and adopting a proactive approach to security, manufacturers and developers can ensure the integrity and safety of embedded systems in various applications.

11.4 Securing IoT Devices with Kali Linux

Kali Linux, a popular penetration testing and ethical hacking distribution, can also be used to enhance the security of IoT devices. While Kali Linux is often associated with offensive security practices, it can be leveraged to assess and secure IoT devices from potential cyber threats. In this section, we will explore how Kali Linux can be utilized to secure IoT devices effectively.

11.4.1 Vulnerability Assessment

Kali Linux provides a wide range of tools for vulnerability assessment and penetration testing. Security professionals can use these tools to identify vulnerabilities in IoT devices and their associated systems. Vulnerability scanning with tools like OpenVAS and Nessus helps detect known weaknesses and misconfigurations that could be exploited by attackers.

11.4.2 Penetration Testing

Ethical hacking using Kali Linux can be employed to conduct penetration testing on IoT devices. By simulating real-world attacks, security professionals can evaluate the resilience of IoT devices against potential cyber threats. This proactive approach helps identify and address vulnerabilities before malicious actors can exploit them.

11.4.3 Firmware Analysis

Kali Linux tools like Binwalk and Firmware Analysis Toolkit (FAT) assist in analyzing the firmware of IoT devices. Security researchers can extract, examine, and reverse engineer the firmware to uncover potential vulnerabilities and security weaknesses.

11.4.4 Network Security

Kali Linux offers various networking tools to assess and secure IoT device communication. Wireshark can be used to capture and analyze network traffic, helping to identify insecure communication practices. By understanding the network traffic patterns, security professionals can detect potential security issues and implement appropriate security measures.

11.4.5 Exploitation Testing

Kali Linux tools, such as Metasploit, can be utilized to conduct exploitation testing on IoT devices. This involves attempting to exploit known vulnerabilities to determine if they can be successfully compromised. By testing for vulnerabilities in a controlled environment, security teams can patch and secure IoT devices before they are deployed.

11.4.6 Password Auditing

Kali Linux includes tools like John the Ripper and Hydra, which can be used to audit passwords on IoT devices. Weak or default credentials are a common entry point for attackers. By conducting password audits, security professionals can identify and enforce stronger password policies.

11.4.7 Secure Firmware Updates

Securing firmware updates is crucial for protecting IoT devices from potential attacks. Kali Linux can be used to assess the security of firmware update mechanisms and ensure they are encrypted and authenticated to prevent tampering.

11.4.8 Implementing Secure Boot

Kali Linux can be used to verify and implement secure boot mechanisms for IoT devices. Secure boot ensures that only trusted and properly signed firmware can run on the device, preventing unauthorized modifications.

11.4.9 Monitoring and Intrusion Detection

Kali Linux can assist in setting up monitoring and intrusion detection systems for IoT devices. Tools like Snort and Suricata can be deployed to monitor network traffic and detect suspicious activities in real-time.

11.4.10 Regular Security Updates

Kali Linux itself receives regular security updates and patches. By keeping Kali Linux up to date, security professionals can benefit from the latest features and improvements while reducing the risk of potential vulnerabilities.

11.4.11 Continuous Security Assessment

IoT security is an ongoing process, and continuous security assessments are crucial. By regularly assessing and updating security measures, organizations can ensure that IoT devices remain protected against emerging threats.

In conclusion, Kali Linux can be a valuable ally in securing IoT devices through vulnerability assessment, penetration testing, and security auditing. By leveraging the powerful tools and capabilities of Kali Linux, security professionals can enhance the overall security posture of IoT devices, protect against potential cyber threats, and contribute to the safe and reliable deployment of IoT technologies.

Chapter 12: Kali Linux in the Cloud

Welcome to Chapter 12 of "The Kali Linux Handbook: A Practical Guide to Advanced Cybersecurity Techniques." In this final chapter, we explore the exciting domain of cloud computing and how Kali Linux can be adapted to address cybersecurity challenges in cloud environments.

The Shift to Cloud Computing

We begin by understanding the paradigm shift to cloud computing and its significance in modern IT infrastructures. As organizations increasingly adopt cloud services, the need to secure cloud environments becomes paramount. In this section, we explore the unique security considerations and risks associated with cloud deployments.

Securing Cloud Infrastructure

In this part, we delve into the methodologies and best practices for securing cloud infrastructure. You'll learn how to leverage Kali Linux tools to assess the security posture of cloud platforms and identify potential vulnerabilities in cloud services and configurations.

Cloud Penetration Testing with Kali Linux

Cloud penetration testing is a specialized skill set crucial for evaluating the resilience of cloud environments against cyber threats. In this section, we explore how to adapt Kali Linux for cloud-based penetration testing. You'll understand the techniques for identifying security weaknesses and misconfigurations specific to cloud services.

Cloud-Based Data Analysis with Kali Linux

Cloud computing offers immense computing power and scalability, making it ideal for data analysis tasks. In this final section, we explore how Kali Linux can be utilized for cloud-based data analysis and cybersecurity research. You'll learn how to harness cloud resources to process large datasets and derive valuable insights for cybersecurity purposes.

Throughout this chapter, we stress the importance of integrating Kali Linux into cloud security strategies. As the cloud computing landscape evolves, understanding how to secure and assess cloud environments is paramount for effective cybersecurity defense.

By mastering Kali Linux in the cloud, you'll be at the forefront of cloud security and equipped to tackle the unique challenges posed by cloud deployments. Let's harness the power of Kali Linux to protect cloud-based services and fortify the future of cybersecurity.

12.1 Deploying Kali Linux on Cloud Platforms

Kali Linux, a popular penetration testing and ethical hacking distribution, can be deployed on various cloud platforms to perform security assessments and conduct ethical hacking tasks in a scalable and flexible manner. Cloud deployment offers several advantages, including on-demand resources, easy scalability, and the ability to access Kali Linux from anywhere. In this section, we will explore how to deploy Kali Linux on cloud platforms and the benefits it provides.

12.1.1 Choosing a Cloud Provider

The first step in deploying Kali Linux on the cloud is to select a suitable cloud provider. Some well-known cloud providers that support Kali Linux deployment include Amazon Web Services (AWS), Microsoft Azure, Google Cloud Platform (GCP), and DigitalOcean. Consider factors such as pricing, available resources, data center locations, and the provider's support for Kali Linux.

12.1.2 Creating a Virtual Machine

Once a cloud provider is chosen, the next step is to create a virtual machine (VM) instance running Kali Linux. This can typically be done through the cloud provider's web-based management console or using command-line tools. During the VM creation process, select the appropriate Kali Linux image or template provided by the cloud provider.

12.1.3 Configuring VM Settings

Configure the VM settings according to the requirements of the security assessments or ethical hacking tasks to be performed. This may include selecting the VM instance type, specifying the amount of RAM and CPU cores, and assigning storage capacity.

12.1.4 Network Configuration

Set up the network configuration for the Kali Linux VM. Assign a public IP address if the VM needs to be accessible from the internet. Additionally, configure network security groups or firewalls to control incoming and outgoing traffic to the VM.

12.1.5 SSH Key Pair

For secure access to the Kali Linux VM, use SSH key-based authentication. Generate an SSH key pair and upload the public key to the cloud provider's console. This ensures that only authorized users can access the VM.

12.1.6 Installation and Updates

Once the Kali Linux VM is deployed, perform initial system setup, including updating the package repositories and installing any required software or tools for the security assessments.

12.1.7 Snapshots and Backups

Cloud platforms often offer snapshot and backup functionalities. Take regular snapshots of the Kali Linux VM to capture its current state, allowing for easy restoration if any issues occur. Additionally, schedule automated backups to protect against data loss.

12.1.8 Monitoring and Logging

Set up monitoring and logging for the Kali Linux VM to track system performance, detect unusual activities, and troubleshoot any potential issues. Use cloud provider-specific monitoring tools or third-party solutions for this purpose.

12.1.9 Data Security

When conducting security assessments on the cloud, it is essential to handle data securely. Encrypt sensitive data, both in transit and at rest, to protect it from unauthorized access.

12.1.10 Compliance Considerations

If the security assessments involve sensitive or regulated data, ensure that the cloud deployment complies with relevant data protection and privacy regulations. Follow industry best practices to safeguard data integrity and confidentiality.

12.1.11 Termination and Cleanup

Once the security assessments are complete, terminate the Kali Linux VM to avoid unnecessary costs. Ensure that any residual data or artifacts are securely removed from the cloud platform.

In conclusion, deploying Kali Linux on cloud platforms provides the flexibility and scalability required for conducting security assessments and ethical hacking tasks. By following best practices for cloud security and proper configuration, organizations can harness the full potential of Kali Linux in the cloud while safeguarding data and ensuring compliance with relevant regulations.

12.2 Conducting Cloud-Based Security Assessments

Cloud-based security assessments offer a powerful and efficient way to evaluate the security of cloud infrastructure, applications, and services. Leveraging cloud resources and tools, security professionals can perform comprehensive assessments to identify and address potential vulnerabilities and risks. In this section, we will explore the process of conducting cloud-based security assessments using Kali Linux or similar tools.

12.2.1 Scope Definition

Before starting the assessment, clearly define the scope of the cloud-based security assessment. Determine the assets and components to be assessed, such as virtual machines, databases, storage, networking, web applications, and identity and access management (IAM) configurations. Clearly outline the goals, objectives, and limitations of the assessment.

12.2.2 Cloud Provider Authorization

Ensure that the cloud provider is aware of and has authorized the security assessment. Some cloud providers have specific terms and conditions regarding security testing on their platforms. Obtain necessary permissions to avoid any potential violations of the cloud provider's policies.

12.2.3 Vulnerability Scanning

Utilize vulnerability scanning tools from Kali Linux or other security testing suites to scan the cloud infrastructure for known vulnerabilities. These tools can assess the security posture of the cloud environment and identify common weaknesses that could be exploited by attackers.

12.2.4 Penetration Testing

Conduct penetration testing on cloud assets to simulate real-world attacks. Use Kali Linux's powerful penetration testing tools to assess the resilience of cloud applications, virtual machines, and services against potential cyber threats. Focus on exploiting vulnerabilities and misconfigurations to gain unauthorized access or escalate privileges.

12.2.5 Web Application Testing

If the cloud environment includes web applications, perform web application testing using tools like Burp Suite, OWASP ZAP, or Nikto. Identify security flaws such as cross-site scripting (XSS), SQL injection, and insecure authentication mechanisms that may exist within the web applications.

12.2.6 Network Security Assessment

Evaluate the network security of the cloud infrastructure by analyzing network traffic, identifying open ports, and reviewing network configurations. Use tools like Nmap, Wireshark, and tcpdump to perform network analysis and detect potential security issues.

12.2.7 IAM and Access Control Review

Assess the effectiveness of identity and access management (IAM) controls in the cloud environment. Ensure that access controls are properly configured, users have the appropriate permissions, and multi-factor authentication (MFA) is enforced where necessary.

12.2.8 Data Security and Encryption

Evaluate data security measures in the cloud environment, including data encryption at rest and in transit. Ensure that sensitive data is properly protected to prevent unauthorized access or data leakage.

12.2.9 Logging and Monitoring

Review logging and monitoring mechanisms in the cloud environment to detect and respond to security incidents effectively. Set up centralized logging and monitoring solutions to track and analyze security-related events.

12.2.10 Secure Configuration Management

Ensure that cloud resources are configured securely according to industry best practices and security standards. Check for misconfigurations that could expose sensitive data or weaken the security posture of the cloud environment.

12.2.11 Compliance Assessment

Assess the cloud environment's compliance with relevant industry standards and regulations, such as GDPR, HIPAA, or PCI DSS. Verify that security controls align with compliance requirements.

12.2.12 Report and Remediation

Compile a comprehensive report detailing the findings, vulnerabilities, and recommendations for remediation. Present the report to the cloud provider's security and IT teams, highlighting critical issues that need immediate attention. Work collaboratively to address the identified security gaps and implement appropriate security measures.

12.2.13 Continuous Monitoring and Improvement

Cloud security is an ongoing process. Establish continuous monitoring and improvement practices to ensure that the cloud environment remains secure over time. Regularly reassess the cloud infrastructure to identify new vulnerabilities and adapt to changing threat landscapes.

In conclusion, conducting cloud-based security assessments with Kali Linux or similar tools allows organizations to proactively identify and address security risks in their cloud environments. By following a systematic approach, leveraging specialized tools, and collaborating with cloud providers, security professionals can enhance the security posture of cloud assets and protect against potential cyber threats.

12.3 Securing Cloud Environments with Kali Linux Tools

Kali Linux offers a wide range of powerful tools that can be utilized to enhance the security of cloud environments. By leveraging these tools, security professionals can identify vulnerabilities, assess risks, and implement robust security measures to protect cloud assets from cyber threats. In this section, we will explore how Kali Linux tools can be used to secure cloud environments effectively.

12.3.1 Vulnerability Assessment

Use vulnerability scanning tools like OpenVAS and Nessus from Kali Linux to regularly scan the cloud environment for known vulnerabilities. Perform thorough vulnerability assessments on virtual machines, databases, web applications, and other components to identify and patch potential weaknesses.

12.3.2 Penetration Testing

Conduct regular penetration testing on cloud assets to test the effectiveness of security controls. Use Kali Linux's powerful penetration testing tools, such as Metasploit, to simulate real-world attacks and evaluate the resilience of the cloud environment against potential threats.

12.3.3 Web Application Security

Kali Linux offers web application security testing tools like Burp Suite and OWASP ZAP. Utilize these tools to identify and remediate security flaws in web applications hosted in the cloud. Focus on vulnerabilities like cross-site scripting (XSS), SQL injection, and insecure direct object references.

12.3.4 Network Security

Assess the network security of the cloud environment using network scanning tools like Nmap and Wireshark from Kali Linux. Identify open ports, review firewall rules, and analyze network traffic to detect potential security issues.

12.3.5 Identity and Access Management (IAM) Review

Review the IAM configurations of the cloud environment to ensure that access controls are appropriately configured. Use Kali Linux tools to audit user permissions, verify multi-factor authentication (MFA) settings, and detect any unauthorized access.

12.3.6 Encryption and Data Security

Evaluate data security in the cloud by checking data encryption measures at rest and in transit. Use Kali Linux to test the strength of encryption protocols and ensure sensitive data is adequately protected.

12.3.7 Logging and Monitoring

Set up centralized logging and monitoring solutions in the cloud environment using Kali Linux tools like ELK stack (Elasticsearch, Logstash, and Kibana). Monitor security-related events to detect anomalies and potential security incidents.

12.3.8 Secure Configuration Management

Implement secure configuration management for cloud resources based on industry best practices. Use Kali Linux tools to perform configuration audits and verify that resources are appropriately configured.

12.3.9 Continuous Security Assessments

Establish a process for continuous security assessments using Kali Linux tools. Regularly scan and test cloud assets to identify new vulnerabilities and address them promptly.

12.3.10 Cloud Security Automation

Automate security tasks in the cloud environment using Kali Linux scripts and tools. This includes automating vulnerability scanning, compliance checks, and security audits to ensure consistency and efficiency.

12.3.11 Incident Response Planning

Develop a robust incident response plan for the cloud environment. Use Kali Linux tools to set up incident response procedures, including data breach analysis and containment strategies.

12.3.12 Training and Awareness

Provide training and awareness programs for cloud users and administrators. Educate them on cloud security best practices and how to leverage Kali Linux tools for security assessments.

12.3.13 Collaboration with Cloud Providers

Collaborate with cloud providers to ensure that security features and controls are effectively implemented and maintained. Stay informed about updates and new security offerings from the cloud provider.

12.3.14 Regular Updates and Patches

Keep the Kali Linux distribution and its tools up to date with the latest security patches and updates. Regularly update the cloud environment with the latest security patches from the cloud provider.

In conclusion, Kali Linux offers a powerful set of tools that can be harnessed to secure cloud environments effectively. By conducting vulnerability assessments, penetration testing, and continuous security monitoring, organizations can enhance the security posture of their cloud assets and protect against potential cyber threats. Regular collaboration with cloud providers and ongoing training for cloud users are essential elements of a comprehensive cloud security strategy.

12.4 Automating Security Testing in the Cloud

Automating security testing in the cloud is essential for maintaining a robust and continuously secure cloud environment. By automating security testing tasks, organizations can efficiently identify and address vulnerabilities, streamline security assessments, and respond promptly to potential threats. In this section, we will explore the benefits of automating security testing in the cloud and how to achieve it using Kali Linux tools and other automation frameworks.

12.4.1 Benefits of Automating Security Testing in the Cloud

Automating security testing in the cloud offers several key benefits:

Efficiency: Automation eliminates the manual effort required for repetitive security testing tasks, saving time and resources.

Consistency: Automated tests ensure that security assessments are performed consistently, reducing the risk of oversight and human error.

Scalability: Cloud environments often involve a large number of assets. Automation allows security testing to scale effortlessly as the cloud environment expands.

Frequent Assessments: Automated testing enables organizations to conduct security assessments more frequently, keeping up with the dynamic nature of cloud environments.

Continuous Monitoring: Automation facilitates continuous monitoring of security controls and configurations, enabling real-time detection and response to security incidents.

Rapid Feedback: Automated security testing provides quick feedback on vulnerabilities and weaknesses, enabling faster remediation.

12.4.2 Automation Frameworks

Several automation frameworks and tools can be used in conjunction with Kali Linux to automate security testing in the cloud:

Ansible: Ansible is a powerful automation tool that allows you to define security tests as code. It can execute security assessments across multiple cloud instances simultaneously.

Terraform: Terraform is an infrastructure-as-code tool that can be used to define cloud resources and configurations. It enables the creation of reproducible cloud environments for security testing.

Jenkins: Jenkins is a popular continuous integration and continuous deployment (CI/CD) automation tool. It can be used to schedule and execute security tests on cloud assets.

OWASP ZAP API: The OWASP ZAP API allows you to automate web application security testing. It can be integrated into CI/CD pipelines to perform continuous security testing on cloud-hosted applications.

Scapy: Scapy is a Python-based tool that allows you to craft and send custom packets on the network. It can be used to automate network security testing in the cloud.

12.4.3 Automated Security Testing Workflow

To implement automated security testing in the cloud using Kali Linux and other tools, follow these steps:

Defining Security Tests: Identify the security tests you want to automate, such as vulnerability scanning, penetration testing, web application testing, and network analysis.

Selecting Automation Frameworks: Choose the appropriate automation frameworks and tools based on your cloud environment and testing requirements.

Infrastructure as Code (IaC): Leverage IaC tools like Terraform to define and provision cloud resources for testing, ensuring consistency and repeatability.

Automated Testing Scripts: Develop automated testing scripts using Kali Linux tools and other security testing tools. Integrate these scripts into the automation framework.

Continuous Integration: Set up continuous integration pipelines using tools like Jenkins to trigger security tests automatically whenever changes are made to the cloud environment.

Scheduled Assessments: Schedule periodic security assessments to run automatically, ensuring continuous monitoring of cloud assets.

Logging and Reporting: Implement logging and reporting mechanisms to capture and analyze test results. Use tools like ELK stack to monitor security events and generate reports.

Integration with Incident Response: Integrate the automated security testing results with your incident response system for prompt action on detected security issues.

12.4.4 Continuous Improvement

Automated security testing should be an iterative process, continuously improving and evolving to meet changing cloud security requirements. Regularly update the automated test scripts, incorporate new security tools, and refine the testing workflows based on feedback and lessons learned.

In conclusion, automating security testing in the cloud using Kali Linux and automation frameworks enhances the efficiency and effectiveness of security assessments. By embracing automation, organizations can proactively identify and address security risks, maintain a continuously secure cloud environment, and respond swiftly to potential threats.

In "**The Kali Linux Handbook: A Practical Guide to Advanced Cybersecurity Techniques**," we embarked on an exhilarating journey through the world of Kali Linux, an indispensable toolkit for cybersecurity professionals and enthusiasts. This comprehensive handbook provided a step-by-step exploration of Kali Linux's powerful tools, methodologies, and real-world applications, equipping readers with the expertise to become skilled defenders of digital landscapes.

From the foundational principles of ethical hacking to advanced network exploitation, each chapter was meticulously crafted to deliver hands-on experience and expert guidance. Readers learned to safeguard critical assets, identify vulnerabilities, and counteract potential cyber threats effectively.

The book began by introducing the significance of Kali Linux in the cybersecurity realm and its role as the premier platform for penetration testing and ethical hacking. Tailored for both beginners and experienced professionals, this handbook catered to diverse levels of expertise, ensuring every reader found value in its pages.

The chapters were designed to build upon one another, providing a seamless learning experience. Ethical considerations were highlighted throughout the book, emphasizing the responsible and lawful use of the powerful techniques discussed.

Readers were empowered with essential skills, including passive and active reconnaissance, vulnerability assessment, wireless network penetration testing, web application security evaluation, and post-exploitation techniques. Additionally, the book delved into advanced Kali Linux tools, IoT and embedded system security, and deploying Kali Linux in cloud environments.

As the journey concluded, readers had honed their abilities to uncover security weaknesses, perform comprehensive network analyses, and respond to security incidents with precision and confidence. They were well-equipped to bolster their organizations' defenses and contribute positively to the ever-changing landscape of cybersecurity.

We hope that "The Kali Linux Handbook" has ignited a passion for ethical hacking and cybersecurity in each reader. Remember, with great power comes great responsibility, and we encourage every reader to use their newfound knowledge for the greater good.

Thank you for joining us on this transformative expedition into the world of Kali Linux and advanced cybersecurity techniques. As the guardians of digital frontiers, let us continue to learn, adapt, and defend against emerging threats, ensuring a safer and more secure digital world for all. May your journey as a cybersecurity expert be both rewarding and fulfilling.

Keep exploring, keep learning, and stay vigilant in the pursuit of cybersecurity excellence. Safe hacking, and may your endeavors be met with success.

Farewell, and until we meet again.

Sincerely,

Oliver O'Neill

Author of "The Kali Linux Handbook: A Practical Guide to Advanced Cybersecurity Techniques"

Printed in Great Britain
by Amazon

41477235R00145